How long were you homeless?

"Six to eight months."

How did you survive?

"Carnegie. Working hard, long hours. I worked over at Lucky Lodge for a little while. Get ten or fifteen dollars over there."

Where do you sleep when there's nowhere to go?

"Could be under the bridge. Could be in the parks, down by the train station. Could be anywhere. The worst place was under the bridge."

What do you think can be done about homeless people?

"Well the first thing is to find some places to get everyone off the street. Drop the rents down, they could possibly do that too. I got a place now over at Lucky Lodge for $220. Fridge and sink and kitchen down the hallway. I only have $183 left over."

Under the Viaduct

Homeless in Beautiful B.C.

SHEILA BAXTER

New Star Books - Vancouver - 1991

Copyright © 1991 by Sheila Baxter

All rights reserved. No part of this work may be reproduced or used in any form or by any means – graphic, electronic, or mechanical – without the prior written permission of the publisher. Any request for photocopying or other reprographic copying must be sent in writing to the Canadian Reprography Collective, Suite M1, 379 Adelaide Street West, Toronto, Ontario M5V 1S5.

First Printing, July 1991
1 2 3 4 5   95 94 93 92 91
Printed and bound in Canada
Printed on acid-free paper

Published by
New Star Books Ltd.
2504 York Avenue
Vancouver, B.C.
V6K 1E3

The article by Keith Chu on page 80 originally appeared in *Artest4*, Summer 1990. The article by Noreen Shanahan on page 184 originally appeared in *Kinesis*, October 1989, and *Pacific Tribune*, November 20, 1989. Both articles reprinted by permission.
All photos are by John A. Cosgrove except: pages 122, 206 by Sheila Baxter; pages 81, 86, Tenants Rights Coalition (TRAC); page 230 by Audrey McClellan
Index: Teresa Murphy
Editor: Audrey McClellan
Cover design: David Lester / Get to the Point ▶ Graphics
Production: Rolf Maurer

The publisher is grateful for assistance provided by the Canada Council and by the Cultural Services Branch, Province of British Columbia

Canadian Cataloguing in Publication Data

Baxter, Sheila, 1933-
    Under the viaduct

    ISBN 0-921586-16-7 (bound). – ISBN 0-921586-15-9 (pbk.)

    1. Homeless persons – British Columbia. 2. Homelessness – British Columbia. 3. Homelessness – Canada. I. Title.
HV4510.B7B39 1991   362.5'09711   C91-091182-7

Contents

Introduction: Homelessness and Political Will   1

Definitions and Causes
What is Homelessness?   7
Why Are People Homeless?   12

Being Homeless
Sheila's Homelessness   21
February   26
The Women   32
March   44
April   53
Interview with a Hotel Manager   63
The Squatters   72
May Day   89
Carnegie Centre—Living Room for the Homeless   99
The Men   103
May   114
Montreal, Toronto, the U.S., and the World   119
June   133
July   145
August   150
September, October, November   157
December   165
The Children   173

Solutions
  Will the Socreds Sell Your Home?   195
  Solutions from the Community   201

Epilogue   215
Bibliography   217
Resources   219
Index   224

To Marguerite D'Youville
To Carnegie members and friends
To New Star and Audrey McClellan
To End Legislated Poverty
To Homeless People all the world over
To Sheila the child within

And to my grandchildren, I leave you the written word. It's all I have...it's valuable...believe me!

Love,

   Grandma

INTRODUCTION:
Homelessness and Political Will

The political will to solve the problem of homelessness is missing in our society. At each level of government throughout Canada, the U.S., and other countries, the politicians throw the ball to each other, trying to fool us with endless committees, studies, papers, media, speeches—each blaming the other for the mess we are in. Developers flip properties for massive profit, and bulldoze low rental units to replace them with expensive condominiums, apartments, offices.

At the same time, interest on loans and mortgages is so high that the majority of young people—and even not-so-young people—will be burdened with huge debts if they buy a house today.

Rents have gone up, but minimum wage isn't enough to rent an apartment, and there is a trend to employ people part time, so they make even less money. The welfare rental allowance still comes nowhere near meeting the cost of accommodation.

On the bright side, the Downtown Eastside Residents Association (DERA) opened some more low income housing, but it hardly makes a dent in the waiting list. This lack of, or loss of, housing is happening in so many cities. Rents are so high that people have to use their food money to pay for shelter; the corporations squeeze us and squeeze us, the government taxes and taxes the workers, and the corporations grow and grow, and pay less and less. Cities of homeless people don't happen by accident.

Is it really the fault of homeless people that they are on the street? Or is it the fault of the system—a system of low-paying jobs, lay-offs, hassles with welfare and unemployment insurance, evictions, hunger, and child apprehension? Did these people choose a life of poverty and homelessness, or did the system break them and push them onto the street?

I am an authority on how it feels to be homeless, the powerlessness and dehumanization of it—because it happened to me. There are people who are homeless by choice, or in their sickness have chosen homelessness, but the involuntary homeless are the majority.

Our society has very limited resources to prevent homelessness, and it too often blames the victim, the poor, the homeless, for the situation in which they find themselves. The shame and the blame build up until the victims turn inward and blame themselves.

This book presents stories and opinions of homeless people, squatters, the evicted, people in shelters, people and families in lousy living accommodation, the sick. It points a big finger away from the victims, towards governments and corporations who control our lives and our living conditions. There are solutions, from people who have researched the problem, and from the homeless themselves.

I think I have met my goals for this book:
- To give a voice to homelessness, to communicate the pain and the long-reaching after-effects on the victims
- To interview people who give services to the homeless, especially through street level and front-line work
- To try and understand the corporate agenda and gentrification of our communities
- To look honestly at my own homelessness, its pain, and to expose parts of me that I've hidden even from myself
- To go back and take a look at Chez Doris and Maison Marguerite, and claim my herstory

This book is set in Vancouver, British Columbia, where I live. But as you read, remember that it's not just a story about Vancouver. The problems are the same everywhere; they are caused by the same trends, and can be attacked with the same solutions.

I went to the groups and workers in Vancouver's downtown eastside, and out of respect for the work they do, I asked their approval to write this book. They were all encouraging, and it was really helpful to have the community's support. My apologies to all the agencies I didn't interview. There are so many (just not enough homes). I've listed some of them in the appendix of cross-Canada services.

Names have been changed, and total anonymity granted when requested. If it's relevant to a situation, e.g. if racism is involved

INTRODUCTION

or when the person interviewed brings it up, I mention if I'm speaking to a person of colour.

I would like to encourage other low-income people to write. Write in your own voice and don't let anyone take your voice away. It's yours, use it!

As of August 1, 1990, welfare rates were raised. The new figures are shown in the table below. Interviewees may refer to earlier rates in the book.

EMPLOYABLE (except single parent families and family members over 60 years old)

Number in family	Support	Max. shelter	Total
1 person	$200	$300	$500
Couple	$352	$485	$837
Couple, 1 child	$423	$560	$983
Couple, 2 children	$494	$600	$1,094
Couple, 3 children	$565	$650	$1,215

UNEMPLOYABLE, single parent families, and people between 60-64

1 Person	$250	$300	$550
Couple, or single parent & child	$402	$485	$887
Family of 3	$473	$560	$1,033
Family of 4	$544	$600	$1,144
Family of 5	$615	$650	$1,265

HANDICAPPED

1 person	$394	$300	$694
2, one handicapped	$546	$485	$1,031
2, both handicapped	$690	$485	$1,175
3, one handicapped	$617	$560	$1,177

SENIORS

1 person (65+)	$394	$300	$694
2, one 65+	$546	$485	$1,031
2, both 65+	$690	$485	$1,175
3, one 65+	$617	$560	$1,177

Definitions and Causes

What is Homelessness?

In his article "Helping and Hating the Homeless" (*Harper's*, January 1990), Peter Marin lists the homeless in American cities: veterans, mainly from the war in Vietnam; the mentally ill; the physically disabled or chronically ill; the elderly on fixed incomes; men, women, and whole families "pauperized by the loss of a job"; single parents, usually women; runaway children; alcoholics and those in trouble with drugs; immigrants, both legal and illegal; traditional tramps, hobos, and transients.

[The homeless] can be elderly or children, single or in families, economically disenfranchised (the poor, chronically or temporarily unemployed and underemployed), or socially marginalized (the mentally ill, physically disabled and chronically ill). Many of them, before they were homeless, were people more or less like ourselves. What now separates them is not so much the presence or absence of shelter, but the lack of a *home*.

They can be divided into two groups: the *absolute* homeless who inhabit the streets by day and either seek refuge at night in emergency shelters or who sleep outside, hiding from the elements and society; and those whose tenuous hold on economic and social stability place them *'at risk'* of becoming homeless. The former are few in number, the latter substantial and growing rapidly.

from "Shelter or Homes: a Contribution to the Search for Solutions to Homelessness in Canada," H. Peter Oberlander and Arthur L. Fallick, from the Centre for Human Settlements, University of British Columbia

Taking homelessness literally, we are talking about a person without a home, without an address, without personal security, without privacy, a person continuously on the move, haunted and hunted, hiding from himself and the personal shame that society has attached to him, or hiding from society as a whole. The proverbial bag-lady, clutching her meagre possessions and shifting from park bench to park bench, and from crowded shelter to crowded shelter, is both reality and a symbol in most Canadian cities. But homelessness is more than a shelter problem. Homelessness is life in disarray.
> H. Peter Oberlander, Director, Centre for Human Settlements, UBC

There seem to be four basic options for defining who the homeless are:
1) people without any shelter on a given night;
2) the first group plus those forced to sleep in temporary shelters;
3) both of the above groups plus those who are forced to live in substandard housing (i.e. housing which seriously violates health and building standards;
4) the above three groups plus those who have to spend an inordinate proportion of their income to obtain decent quality housing, such that other aspects of living, such as proper diet, are seriously affected.
> from "Who Are the Homeless? What is Homelessness?", a paper presented by David Hulchanski and Arthur Fallick to the Conference on Homelessness in B.C., May 1987

Homelessness is the condition of low-income people who cannot find adequate, secure housing at a price they can afford. The most obvious element of homelessness is the lack of housing; but just as "home" is more than physical shelter, "homelessness" includes a lack of this base for the rest of life's activities. "Home" is associated with personal identity, family, relationships, a role in the community, privacy and security, and the possession of personal property. Homelessness or the lack of a home affects all these areas of an individual's life.
> from "The Case for Long-Term, Supportive Housing," a paper by the Single Displaced Persons' Project, Toronto

WHAT IS HOMELESSNESS?

Homelessness in Canada is the absence of a continuing or permanent *home* over which individuals or family groups have personal control and which provides the essential needs of shelter, privacy and security at an affordable cost, together with ready access to social and economic public services.
from "Shelter or Homes," H. Peter Oberlander and Arthur L. Fallick

We got our definition of homelessness from the UN. The definition we use is: anyone who doesn't have security of tenure in the place they're living. Meaning, anyone who's not secure where they're living, and it can disappear at any time, which is basically anyone who's living in a hotel down here [Vancouver's downtown eastside], even though they're now covered under the Residential Tenancy Act. A lot of hotel owners still don't recognize that, and still toss people out in the middle of the night. If you're living under a fear that, if you go to a manager and say "I don't have any heat," the man's going to kick you out, that is not security of tenancy, that's homelessness. So in our community, we have about 10,000 people who are homeless.

Another example is when you have a family living in a hotel. Now they don't go, "Oh, when we grow up we're going to have a family and live in a hotel." There's no way anyone dreams of that sort of stuff. There might be a junkie down the hall, a drunk puking in a hallway. You've got one toilet and one bath to service thirty rooms. These are really rough places. Families shouldn't be in there. Sometimes families are split. They have rooms on different floors. All they're doing is a holding pattern until they can find a decent place to live.

The image we get on American television all the time is under the bridges and stuff, and people think you're only homeless if you're under a bridge. We use the term shelterless. If they're shelterless, they're under a bridge—but you can be homeless living inside a building. People can live twenty years in the same room and be terrified that at any moment they can be tossed out, for no reason, through intimidation and through all sorts of stuff. Until they have secure housing, which is one of the things social housing does provide, that's the definition we should be looking at,

not people that are in the street. That's what people would like to think—we don't have a homeless problem because we don't have people sleeping in my doorway. But we have a homeless problem because we have people in hotels, who don't have decent housing.
    Stephen Learey, Downtown Eastside Residents Association (DERA)

[Homelessness refers to] the millions of people with no home—the pavement dwellers, those who must sleep in doorways, subways, and recesses of public buildings and those rendered homeless by natural and man-made disaster, but also the hundreds of millions who lack a real home—one which provides protection from the elements; has access to safe water and sanitation; provides for secure tenure and personal safety; is within easy reach of centres of employment, education and health care; and is at a cost which people and society can afford. Shelter is a global issue. It is not simply an issue of poverty. Urbanization, economic development and social policies all have direct effects on shelter conditions, and must be addressed.
    United Nations Centre for Human Settlements (Habitat)

"Adequate shelter" must be recognized as being more than four walls and a roof: at the very least adequate shelter also includes security of tenure/occupation, and reasonable access to infrastructure, basic services and employment. Governments are therefore urged to recognize that "human settlements" cannot be regarded as merely a sectoral activity in national development plans. Human settlements are the final product in terms of built/living environments of all sectoral activities.
    from "International Year of Shelter for the Homeless," by Ingrid Munro, in Cities: The International Quarterly on Urban Policy *4 (1987)*

Comments from street people:
    "Homeless was having money for booze but none for a room when I was drunk."
    "I slept in a friend's hotel room in the day, then left it when he

came home. I had no money for rent so I stayed out at night, slept in the day."

"My hotel room is homeless."

"I panhandled one time—couldn't make enough for a room, just a little for booze."

"Homeless is knowing you can be evicted any time."

"Homelessness is always having to move on."

"Homelessness is being forced to move out of your community."

"Homelessness is having your home bulldozed."

"Homelessness is rent increases that force you out."

"Homelessness is getting well after you've had a relapse to find all your stuff has been trashed."

"Homelessness is being apprehended."

"Homelessness is when you come out of jail and you don't know where you belong."

"Homelessness is not knowing where to go."

"Homelessness is when the plant closes and your bank forecloses your mortgage."

Why Are People Homeless?

Income problems: no money.
Work-related problems: no job, no training, no prospects, seasonal and chronic unemployment.
Health-related problems: no access to vital services, deteriorating physical and mental health.
Family/relationship problems.
Housing problems: no access to affordable, adequate, secure housing.

The main precipitants of homelessness in Canada include:
 1) Unemployment, underemployment and unemployability
 2) Poverty
 3) Lack of affordable housing
 4) The breakdown of the traditional family structure
 5) Inadequacies and inequities in the provision of social welfare
 6) Lack of diversified community support systems for the deinstitutionalized
 7) Displacement occasioned by urban revitalization.
   "Homelessness and the Homeless" by H. Peter Oberlander and Arthur L. Fallick, UBC

There is growing consensus that homelessness in Canada is attributable in part to the organization of the housing market. Evidence suggests that there are increasing numbers of people who require low rent, permanent and secure accommodation at a time when the stock of appropriate types of affordable housing is diminishing.
   from "Shelter or Homes," by H. Peter Oberlander and Arthur L. Fallick

Poverty creates homelessness
End Legislated Poverty, July 1990

A single person in B.C. can work full time at the minimum wage and will end up nearly $3000 per year below the poverty line.

In 1975 a person working full time at the minimum wage earned 122 percent of the poverty line. Today that person would have to earn $7.50 an hour to reach 122 percent of the poverty line.

Between 1981 and 1986 Stats Canada found that jobs paying $5.24 or less increased much faster than jobs paying more.

The Bank of Canada admits to purposely keeping interest rates high so that unemployment will be high so that wages will fall. They call this their "anti-flation" strategy. But low-paid workers pay the price of poverty.

Real average earnings in the Greater Vancouver Regional District have declined in the last year by over $5 a week.

Over 126,000 British Columbians are officially unemployed (Stats Canada, June 1990). Stats Canada's definition of someone

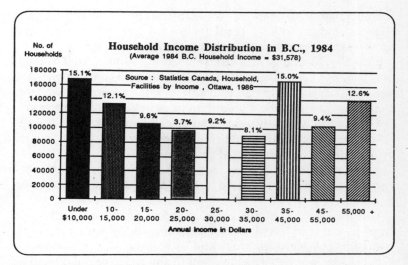

Source: *A Place to Call Home.*

who is "employed" includes people who have worked one hour per week.

The Economic Council of Canada says that job growth in Canada is split between good jobs and bad jobs. The bad jobs are in the low-paid service sector where increases in minimum wage would make a big difference.

A Canada Employment study predicts that most of the jobs in 1995 in B.C. will be in the low-paid service sector. They will be jobs as sales clerks, secretaries, waiters, cashiers, and janitors.

Between December 1980 and January 1987, the Socred government froze B.C.'s minimum wage at $3.65 per hour. If they had increased it with inflation, it would now be over $7 per hour.

To escape poverty, one person would have to earn $6.53 an hour to support herself; $8.62 an hour to support two people; $11.53 an hour to support three people; and $13.28 an hour to support four people. This does not include payroll deductions or childcare costs, and is based on a 37.5 hour week.

Homelessness: Documenting its increase through the Tenants Rights Coalition

The information listed below was gathered primarily through the Tenants Rights Hotline, April 1989-April 1990, during a rental housing crisis of monumental proportions.

Canadian Mortgage and Housing Corporation (CMHC) statistics, October 1989, found Vancouver with a .3 percent vacancy rate. The crisis also spread into surrounding communities, thus dispelling the myth that "if you can't live in Vancouver, then you can always move to (Burnaby, Surrey, Richmond, etc.)."

Furthermore, the affordable rental housing stock—particularly in Vancouver—is being lost at an alarming rate, through demolition and conversion into luxury condominiums (over 1000 units lost over a three month period in 1989) and this stock is not being replaced.

Vancouver's downtown eastside hotels, traditionally the "last stop" in terms of rental accommodation, are presently showing "no vacancy" signs as well, and an estimated 1500 units are expected to face the wrecking ball in the next couple of years.

WHY ARE PEOPLE HOMELESS?

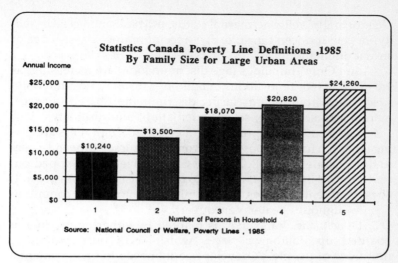

Source: *A Place to Call Home.*

Below are a number of observations we've recently made in situations where tenants are either finding their homes threatened, or are in fact finding themselves without a home.

The list is in no particular order.

1. *Evictions.* There are three main types of eviction: a) non payment of rent; b) cause; c) landlord use. There has been a marked increase in evictions for "non payment of rent," translated to mean more and more tenants unable to pay the high rents now demanded.

There has also been an increase in evictions for "cause." This ties in closely with tenant-harrassment by landlords, and the fact that many landlords seem to consider tenants to be dispensable.

Finally, evictions for "landlord use" are also increasing. Landlords are demolishing, renovating extensively, or moving their families into a previously rented suite. The result: homelessness, sometimes faced by tenants who had lived in a suite and paid rent monthly for years.

2. *Harrassment.* Inflicted on tenants by landlords, particularly on women or tenants actively standing up for their (tenant) rights. (In some cases, we've heard cases of sexual harrassment.)

3. *Discrimination.* The present B.C. Human Rights Act prohibits discrimination in tenancies on the basis of: race, colour, ancestry,

place of origin, religion, marital status, physical or mental disability, or sex. It doesn't include age, receipt of public assistance or sexual orientation.

"Adult Only" buildings (age discrimination) are increasing, as are evictions for renovations in buildings turned into adult only. Also heard from tenants facing discrimination based on: race, marital status, income, sexual orientation, and disability.

4. *Rent increases.* As previously mentioned, high rents are giving tenants a further boost away from housing security and closer to homelessness. The B.C. Social Credit government wiped out rent controls in 1984 and refuses to re-establish them. As a result, 30 percent rent increases are becoming common (in all communities throughout Greater Vancouver).

5. *Demolitions.* Vancouver is marked by either empty lots or boarded up buildings; places which were once homes to hundreds of people. A developer only needs to give a tenant a two month termination notice, and have the "intent" to demolish, to empty out a building.

6. *Squatting.* One result of the housing crisis is squatting; tearing down the boards and making a deserted building into a place to live when no other is available.

7. *Secondary Suite Closure.* Further loss of affordable rental housing and intimidating to tenants living there.

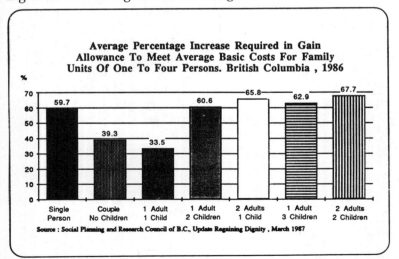

Source: *A Place to Call Home.*

WHY ARE PEOPLE HOMELESS?

8. *Mobile Homes.* Mobile home park lands are being redeveloped, which forces tenants off the land. It's tremendously expensive to move these mobile homes, and less land is available upon which to move them.

9. *Women and physical abuse.* Due to the tight rental market, we're hearing from more women who are choosing to remain in a violent home rather than risk losing a home. (This is especially apparent where children are involved.)

10. *Emergency Women's Shelters filled.* More women are unable to move from these shelters, due to the fact that they can't locate housing.

11. *Doubling Up.* More shared accommodation; single mothers, especially, are sharing expenses by sharing their homes. Several problems might result from this: increased harrassment by landlord; eviction for overcrowding; rent increases; lack of living space; possible loss of tenant rights (if person is a "licensee" instead of a legally recognized tenant).

Being Homeless

Sheila's Homelessness

War... something adults were talking about, whispering. A six-year-old girl picked up fear as the words of war were spoken. It was London, England, and war had started.

I knew Hitler had a mustache and that he was a bloody awful man. I was a cockney kid and really swore quite well for my age. I knew I was going somewhere. I had a little bag and was queuing up with all the other kids. I was one of the smallest. The headmaster, a short chubby man, Mr. Gossling he was called, picked me out for a kiss and a big squeeze goodbye. I was about to become homeless.

For a while I was in a nice home. Then one night someone came and I was moved to an abandoned laundry with at least fifty other children who were unwanted and homeless. In a large room, campcots were lined side by side, row on row. I always had trouble finding mine; they all looked alike and seemed to stretch forever.

There was one sink with a cold water tap, no bath, just splash water on your hands and that was the daily routine. Of course most of the children became covered in scabies and lice, impetigo. We couldn't go to school. I guess we were the untouchables. The intense hunger and sadness I felt was shared with the other children, but all we talked about was the hunger.

I remember I would pounce with joy on any food I found on the street, even though it was dirty: discarded apple cores, a crust of bread, or cabbage leaves left on plants. Scraping up chewing gum from the road, we would fight over it, even though it was black.

I remember it was so cold we huddled around an old black stove. I went into a farmer's field and found a couple of shrivelled potatoes. I tried to roast them on the stove and badly burned my fingers. I don't remember anyone taking care of it. The burn became full of pus.

Later I recall being stood naked in a tin bath. The water was so cold. Someone was scrubbing my sores with a brush. It hurt, but I didn't cry. I knew I was homeless, I just didn't know why. I learned to accept the pain, the hunger. It was my life and I was powerless. I was just a child and adults were to be obeyed, listened to. I understand the powerlessness of people who have given up. Sometimes that's the only way to survive when there isn't a way out. You just do what you have to do, day by day, and try to stay alive.

I was about 11 years old, a sad, scruffy kid crying myself to sleep every night, praying to god to send someone to love me, someone to save me.

She came home drunk from the pub, as she did most times. I awoke to her running up the stairs, cursing me. She yanked me out of bed, hitting and smashing me about the head and face, telling me I was going to die and that I should pray because she was going to kill me. As she held the knife at my throat, I remember clearly how calm I was. She had done this before, many times. I just thought survival. How could I escape? I asked to go to the lavatory. It worked...

I ran down the stairs, grabbing a coat and some shoes from the small hallway. I can see the door now as I desperately grabbed for the lock, hoping I could make it out the door before she caught me. When I got out, I ran and ran, the thought "escape escape" running through my brain. The night's darkness and the cold was safety.

I went to the Tube station. It was closed, but a little warmer. No one would help me. The neighbours were scared of my mother, and so were my father's relatives. I had no place to go. A policeman came round the corner. He caught me and took me to the police station. They questioned me, but I wouldn't give them my name or address. I was scared they would take me back. They put me in a cell deep below the ground. It was so hot I thought I would suffocate. There was a red rubber mattress on the floor. The door had a small square in it; someone would look through it once in a while. I felt terror at being in the jail cell, but to go home was even worse.

Eventually, next day, I gave in and told them where I lived.

They took me back. My mother was sober by then, and they believed her when she said that I was just a bad kid.

I made sure the police never caught me again. When I ran to survive, I stayed hidden.

Children run from abuse like I did. They learn it's safer to stay hidden. The danger of homelessness is less frightening than the abuse in the home. This is hard to write. It opens scars, brings out feelings of shame, of wondering "what will people think of me?" But it is written to help the reader understand how the street can be the only choice some children can make.

I empathise with kids that are homeless. I've been there. I empathise with adults who were abused, homeless children. Just remember it wasn't our fault. Get rid of the shame.

I was 21, pregnant. In 1955 there was less than zero housing anywhere in London for rent. We lived in one of the last gas-lit houses in London: there was no electricity. I can never forget that house. It was so dark and damp. It was near Blackheath where the black plague victims of London were buried—a frightening place to live, but we had no choice at the time. We had a room in the basement to sleep and live in, a little scullery to cook in. The gas light wasn't in the lavatory or the narrow dark hallway.

I was about six months pregnant and I went to pee in the lavatory. It was dark. I heard a loud squeal from the toilet bowl as I sat down on it. A rat bit my ass. I screamed and screamed as I ran up the dark hallway. My husband killed it with a hammer—it was a large sewer rat.

The baby was born. We had no bathroom, no bath, no hot water. There was nowhere to live. So we emigrated to Canada to find a place to live.

We had moved to Selby Street below the tracks in Montreal Westmount. I'm not sure of the exact date—1965, 1966. My first daughter had some medical problems so we moved to be nearer the children's hospital. Medicare wasn't in place yet, and we depended on the clinic.

My husband (we were still married then), five children, and I moved into a huge old flat. It was really cheap and the train tracks ran outside the back yard. Everything in the kitchen started to rock when the trains sped through. Kids liked waving to the train drivers. I was happy there. Then, bang... we got eviction notices.

The government was expropriating for the Trans-Canada Highway.

It was a small, intimate street; we all knew each other. Two elderly sisters lived in the house they had been born in. Everyone was upset about the evictions. We protested. So the government hired a woman, put her in one of the empty flats, and called her a relocation service. All she did was read the ads in the paper and send people to places that had been rented. But it looked good in the papers. Years after, they did build a few low-cost rentals somewhere else, but I'm sure not too many of the original tenants got into them.

I was so angry at the way we were expropriated for that damned highway. But of course we moved again.

It was Vancouver, 1980, and my house had just burned down.

After the fire someone took us to a hotel for two days. I was in shock, numb. I remember we had the kittens with us, but I can't remember what happened to them. Then I was given a pair of men's runners at least five sizes too big, and some clothes that were too small. Someone came to take us to the YWCA. I had to walk down a crowded lunch hour street. I felt so humiliated; I wanted to tell everyone, "Hey, this isn't the real me! I just lost everything in a fire."

My sons stayed together at my eldest son's small apartment. There was no room for my two daughters and me, so we were taken to the YWCA, to their hotel. The room was clean and bright, there were three beds. I wasn't functioning well; I was still in shock.

We had come to Vancouver to join my eldest son just six months before. I had used up my savings on the transportation, shipping belongings and furnishing the house on Charles Street. I was on UI. Now there was no housing to be found, jobs were scarce. People helped look for a rental. There was nothing. Some kind people tried to salvage some of my possessions. I couldn't stand the smell of the smoke on them. It just made me cry. I was feeling like my world had caved in, depressed, powerless. When a YWCA worker explained to me that we would have to vacate the room because they needed to rent it for money, that they couldn't afford for me to stay there any longer, it had been less than two weeks since the fire.

I felt humiliation flood my soul. Somehow I started to blame myself for my homelessness. I couldn't get help from welfare because I was on UI, so what could I do? In the eastside some money had been collected in trust for the Eastside Family Place. I told them to keep it as an emergency fund for someone with emergency need. I didn't take any of it.

Friends in Montreal sent me some money and I went back to Montreal with my youngest daughter and two shopping bags of possessions, leaving my teenage children behind because they had jobs. I knew I would just burden them down. As I waved my family goodbye at the airport, I cried and cried, I loved them so much. I was powerless, no options, scarcely functioning. I figured I was doing the right thing.

In Montreal, the pain of leaving my family never left. It only started to heal when my eldest son got married and said, "Mom, you've got to come back. You're going to be a grandmother and we want you around when the baby's born." There was an easier rental market by that time.

You can't turn the clock back, what's past is past. The terror and misery that homelessness brings are hell. It took so long for me to recover. What I needed at the time was a home, furniture, counselling, a job...They just weren't available. I gave up the struggle and went back to Montreal and lived on welfare. Society often judges homeless people as drunks, druggies, and non-deserving people. I say that every human being is an individual and must be treated for individual needs. Homelessness and poverty are not a personal problem but a social problem. One solution would be to stop blaming the victim.

February

Ralph Buckley, Strathcona Community Health Team

Ralph Buckley has been collecting statistics on the actual homeless, not those in shelters, waiting for somewhere to live, or in downtown hotel rooms.

"In terms of the shelterless on the street, it's my observation we do not have a large population of people living in the streets. And of that population, from the [homeless] survey we have done, maybe 15 to 20 percent of those would be mentally ill. It's hard to say, it's not that precise an instrument. You go from there to the downtown eastside hotels, and there's a significant population of mentally ill clients in downtown eastside hotels, like the Ohio Rooms that burned down, the Balmoral, the Washington—the downtown eastside hotels are like anything else: some are not too bad, others are lousy.

"But what I'm saying is, these people are not in the streets. A lot are in hotels. They could be in better accommodation than what they are in. They are in shelters like Lookout, Cordova House, and that sort of thing. These are much fuller than they should be.

"What we do know, and what is of serious concern, is that people are being turned away. Where they eventually wind up...If you talk to Crosswalk (the sit-up), they're fairly full, but they're not full to overflowing. Triage is down and then up. You get a varied picture. When the final report comes out it will more or less state that we are in a situation where we appear overall to be sort of holding the line.

"But that delicate balance could easily change with more hotels closing down. Where do these people go? I don't know. Maybe they're moving to New Westminster, Port Coquitlam, Whalley. It's not clear. But I maintain they are not *yet* in the streets to any significant number. You get one, two, five, ten—but not in significant numbers, nothing in comparison to Seattle, Portland.

"The concerns for the clients we have are that they are in substandard hotels. It would be good to get them into better accommodation. This is not that easy to do. You can get them into subsidized housing. There are mental health boarding homes and that. Occasionally you get a vacancy. The difficulty with some of these individuals is they don't wish to move. It's not a simple matter of having a place for them to go. Many are paranoid, distrustful, they do not like rules and regulations, which inevitably come with subsidized housing, and they don't fit. So there's a complexity of problems.

"Many of them can not fit into the housing projects and that, just because of unusual behaviour, disorganized thought process, and that sort of thing. It requires some facility that has a commitment and an understanding. I don't see that being done

privately. If it is done privately, it would be organized through the government, so it would wind up being a government service one way or the other. The marketplace itself would just not be interested in the kind of people we need to provide a service to."

Shelterless Committee Newsletter
January 1990

Reporting agencies: DERA, Lookout, Vancouver Detox Centre, Vancouver General Hospital, Vancouver Police Department, Triage

Male	Female	Total
40	2	42

Where Sleeping
Unknown   24
Outside/streets   24
Under bridge   2
Kits Beach   1
Oppenheimer Park   1
Pigeon Park   1
Carroll & Cordova   1
Raymur & Venables   1
Doorways   1
Restaurant   1

Reasons
Unknown   13
Lack of money   13
Alcoholism—drank rent money 6
Alcoholism   2
Illegal hotel eviction   2
No welfare money   2
No place to stay   1
Lack of money, transient   1
Drug user—spent money   1
Drug abuse   1
People stole from her   1

Average age: 39
Age Range: 22 to 75

Comments
Unkempt 4
Lying on sidewalk 3
No home/nowhere to sleep 2
Unkempt/malnurtured 2
Sick 1
Suffers from emphysema 1
Glue sniffer 1

Severe laceration of face due to seizure 1
Spent all his money on presents for his kids 1
Lookout kicked out for selling drugs 1
MSSH won't help 1
Needs medical attention for stab wounds 1
Has hepatitis 1
Depressed 1
Finds shelter (usually hospital) when cold weather approaches 1
Comes to hospital requesting shelter 1
Suicidal 1
Well kept 1

Anecdotal comments from reporting agencies:

Catholic Charities
Tom Farrell reports business as usual, no change; still running at 100 percent occupancy.

Crosswalk
Lawrence O'Reilley reports they have the "regular amount" of clients. At night their sofas are usually full and a few individuals sit at the table. On average there are six people on the sofas and about five at the table. With women they occasionally place four or five a night in their upstairs section. Mr. O'Reilley observed that they seem to be seeing quite a few young people in their teens.

Al Armstrong reports that their day program has about a 20 percent increase. They see lots of transient people and also an increase in substance abuse.

DERA
DERA reports a large number of illegal hotel evictions since November (31), the beginning month of the shelterless survey. Laura Stannard reports that they believe there are many illegally evicted hotel tenants who are unable to access themselves into Social Services and who end up shelterless for the night. It seems that despite recent amendments to the Residential Tenancy Act, hotel tenants' rights continue to be ignored. It seems that the Residential Tenancy Branch has not informed hotel owners of the new amendments, and as a result, enforcement of the legislation is extremely difficult. With an illegal eviction, an Order of Posses-

sion can be obtained by the tenant but if the landlord still refuses to allow the tenant access, the complications increase exponentially. The police have no jurisdiction in a provincial law. A Writ of Possession, obtained through the Supreme Court, is needed, along with a bond of several hundred dollars, before a sheriff will intervene. Few hotel tenants have the means to see this process through. DERA feels strongly that the current Residential Tenancy Act does not adequately protect tenants from the possibility of being shelterless at a moment's notice.

Downtown Eastside Youth Activities Society
John Turvey reports that there are a number of individuals who stay up all night and then sleep in different resources during the day. At their facility during the day the couches are always filled with two to four people sleeping. John felt also that the weather could be a factor.

The Door is Open
The staff at the Door is Open stated that they notice they are seeing more and more people and that a number of them are without shelter. Furthermore, a lot of them are younger people than previously, in the age range of 20 to 30.

Downtown Health Clinic
Jeff Brooks reports that although their overall statistics are up, they see nothing noticeable with respect to the shelterless.

Dunsmuir House
Mr. Taylor reports that January was a very busy month. On Sunday, January 4, they turned away 30 people.

Dugout
Roy Covenay reports that Dugout has been quite quiet in January. They did not see anyone who appeared shelterless. They also did not see anyone with sleeping bags.

First United Church
Alan Alvare reports that in January they had many requests for sleeping bags and when they ran out of sleeping bags, the individuals then asked for blankets. The soup kitchen stats for January were 2755, up 750 from January 1989.

Long House Council of Native Ministry

Barry Morris reported that some of the places where people slept overnight have been closed off. At Cordova and Powell, for instance, the Port Authority and the CPR wired off a section where people used to sleep out. It was a kind of campground of lean-tos where four to ten people would sleep at any one time. Mr. Morris made the observation that many people are *doubling and tripling up in hotel rooms*.

Lookout

Lookout had 80 *documented* turn-aways in January (67 male and 13 female). Karen O'Shannacery reports that they are seeing more teenagers, ages 16 to 18.

Ministry of Social Services and Housing (MSSH) Bed Index

Judy Hays reports that their volume of requests varies enormously. If all hostel beds in the city are full then they provide alternate accommodation. This applies to those on income assistance as well as those with an appointment but no interim finances. So far, they have not encountered a night when there were no beds to be had anywhere.

Triage

Triage had 36 turn-aways in January (28 male and 8 female). Triage staff reported that the pressure seems to have eased off a bit in January. They theorize that perhaps with the bad weather people secured more permanent housing. January was the lowest occupancy rate they have had for a year.

Vancouver Detox Centre

Diane Wenham reports any homeless people they are seeing are younger, in their late 20s or early 30s. They are also dealing with a lot more transient people from the Prairies, Ontario and Quebec.

Vancouver General Hospital

VGH was very busy in January. Helen Stannard reports that at one point they had 10 patients over their bed count who were placed in medical emergency.

The Women

At the Downtown Eastside Women's Centre I ran into some old friends—a couple of women who had told their stories in my last book. One said, "I took a homeless person to my hotel room. I had a couple of dollars in my purse. In the morning she was gone and so was my money." The other woman, a real motherly type, said, "I help the homeless. I met this young man, he was backpacking and he didn't have any money and I showed him Gastown and other places, then I helped him find a hostel."

We women were sitting around a white arborite table, drinking weak coffee (it was free), swapping stories, just like women in Shaughnessy do I guess. One said, "You know there was once a time when I was homeless and I had to have sex with a man. I just wanted a clean bed with sheets on it. I was homeless. I had no choice," she whispered. "No choice. I didn't know the resources."

Another woman, Tracy, a single parent, said, "I've just been homeless for eight months. It was hell on my children. One threatened suicide." Tracy was nervous, shaky, a woman who was trying to recover from being homeless. She wanted to tell her story in my book, she said, but as we taped she kept breaking down, her hands covering her face. She was an intelligent, warm, kind person. I told her about my homelessness and we shared stories and shared the pain. Tracy plans to go back to school and continue her education.

Tracy

"When I left the relationship I went into a women's shelter with my five children. I was there for about two and a half months, and two of my children had problems in the shelter. I had no place to go and the social services said if I didn't find a place soon, I was going to be cut off welfare. I ended up moving out of the shelter into the YWCA. I was there for a month and a half. During that time my worker kept threatening to cut my welfare off unless I found a home.

"I was trying to find a place since... even before I left the relationship. It was difficult. Most landlords don't want to have single mothers or mothers on welfare, or because I had too many children, they would not accept me.

"During that time, two of my kids... it really hit them hard. And I had to send them away. I was in a state of panic. And two of my kids couldn't handle being homeless. I didn't know what else to do, you know. I sent two back east to stay with my mom. I was really confused. I felt really bad because I couldn't provide a home for my children. I must have seen hundreds of houses.

"In the end I moved back in with the person who abused me because I had nowhere else to go. I had full intentions of moving back out as soon as I found a place, but I didn't find one. I stayed two and a half months. It reached a head again where the abuse was getting worse and worse and worse. I couldn't take it anymore. This time I had three kids. I left again to go into a shelter. And I met another woman there who had also been in an abusive relationship and who needed to find a place. She also had a number of children. So we went looking for a whole entire house rather than a suite, because it was easier to rent a house. We'd seen quite a few before any of them would accept us. We've got one now; I've got the basement suite, she's got the upstairs suite.

"I haven't recovered from it yet. I'm trying to get my life back into order. I couldn't do anything during the time I was homeless. I couldn't make commitments to anybody. I wanted to go to school. I wanted to volunteer some place, at some women's centres. I couldn't do these things. My whole life was on hold. You're totally powerless. Everybody makes decisions for your life without even consulting you, like social services. They just make decisions for you. The solutions to my problems would have been emergency housing, not a shelter.

"My definition of homeless is any person who doesn't have a place to call their own. Doesn't have their own sink. Anytime you feel obliged to someone else. Then it's not your home.

"I really don't know if my present housing is temporary. I hope it's okay. I'm hoping to get into a co-op. Or social housing. I don't know if I'm going to bring my children back. I'm really worried about bringing them back. They went through almost a nervous breakdown. It was extremely difficult. It's hard on kids. One of them tried to jump out of the window of the shelter. I had to fight social services to keep them in their regular school because they needed some stability. I had a real hard time with social services when I was trying to get bus passes. I think social services gave me a hard time because they just wanted to get me out of their office, out of their hair.

"Social services blame you for your homelessness. When you can't find a house it's your fault. They blame you for situations you have no control over. When you come from an abusive relationship it's your fault. When anything goes wrong it's your fault. They make you feel that way by telling you over and over again: It's your fault, it's your fault, it's your choices. My worker says it's my choices, but I didn't have any choices. I did what I could to survive. I took what was available. There are no choices.

"I've noticed that other women I have spoken to, that have been homeless and in shelters, it takes a long time to recover. I don't know if I ever will recover. I know one woman that said after two years she was just starting to recover. And during that time I lost two children, I had to send them away. I don't know how this is going to affect my children later on, the long term effect.

"When I got my basement suite I was ecstatic. I couldn't believe it, after being homeless for so long. My own cupboards. It was mine. My own place, my own washroom. No matter how bad it looked, it was mine. I don't care how bad and decrepit the place is, it's mine. It's home. I'm crying because after being homeless for eight months, it's like a miracle."

Hank, a community worker who is also a musician, told me about one night when he was working late at a community centre. The staff was called because a woman with an obvious mental problem was lifting up her skirt. She had no underwear on, so was exposing herself. Hank went to talk to her. She was homeless, didn't have a place to stay. She asked Hank, "Will you take me home?" She was very sick, but even in her sickness she knew that staying on the street was dangerous, that she would probably get raped or beaten. She was desperately seeking refuge the only way she knew how.

In Montreal in the 1970s I worked with homeless women. It was the same then: women scared of social workers, scared of institutions, homeless, poor, sick, were surviving by giving up their bodies for a place to sleep. I'm happy that there are many more shelters today and that if you have an address you can get welfare, but so many fall through the cracks—the craters!

Where do homeless transsexuals go? What drop-in centre can they use? What shelter do they go to? The women's centre has a policy of no men. Women who are fleeing abuse want a safe refuge and are entitled to it. So the transsexuals couldn't go there. They were asked to leave. They can't go to men's shelters wearing dresses. They often feel they are women but are trapped in men's bodies. Some are in the sex trade; some aren't. They have a hard time finding accommodation. The community has given some money for them to have their own drop-in centre. The bottom line is: everyone should have the option of a space to call their own.

Melanie

I met Melanie, a woman of colour, at the Downtown Eastside Women's Centre. She had volunteered to make baked beans for everyone. I knew her a couple of years ago. She had changed. Then she was much happier, more aggressive, and had great dreams and was optimistic about her future. This day she was much quieter. The poverty-housing syndrome gets to you after a while.

"My definition of homelessness is a failure to find (does it exist?) affordable housing to fill your personal needs, i.e. safe, clean, handicapped accessible, yard for kids, close to schools, etc. It's no good to get 'a place' if you're scared to go home at night because the people upstairs are violent, fighting drunks or junkies, being scared to move because you are a visible minority single mom on welfare with two kids and *no one* wants to rent to you. A house, a home is somewhere you feel safe, put down roots, have a garden, sit in the yard, *not* where you are afraid of eviction for bogus or development reasons. Homelessness is being in transition every two years or less. I have been homeless three times with two kids.

"Housing that fits within my welfare budget—I always pay at least $50 to $100 over my rent money. That extra comes from my food money. That explains why so many more people need the food banks now. You *must* have a place to live, a roof over your head, it rains a lot here, you know? If you have to spend two-thirds of your money on rent, then you know that next month you will be doing the rounds to feed your family, Salvation Army, First United, and if you don't mind a note on your file saying that you don't know how to budget money, go and grovel to your worker. All of this is tiring and drains you of any enthusiasm for life."

To the Bag Lady on Main and 18th

You sleep in the doorways
near Main and 18th
the Safeway cart
your home on wheels
filled with
endless bags
They tell me you choose
this life
I want to visit
but you prefer your
aloneness
When I'm home in bed, warm
I think about you
In the morning
I see you with your cart
sheltering
at the bus stop
Bag lady...what's going to
happen to you?

Cathy

Cathy is a small woman, thin, pale, with a gentle, soft voice. She's close to fifty, comes from a middle-class family, and has a university degree. She carries her possessions with her: not a huge amount, just one backpack. She always looks clean and well-dressed, in simple clothes. She probably owns a couple of pairs of pants, a sweater, and one or two sweat shirts, and has a pair of walking shoes for summer.

Cathy functions well for a while in a hotel or a rooming house, and then her sickness comes on and she screams and rants and breaks things, and the rages get violent. She is hospitalized, then it's back to the street, a hotel, eviction again, the street, and homelessness. She sometimes stays with a man and has frequently been abused.

We talk often together of men and love and painful relationships, and about doctors and workers who don't really understand her pain. She doesn't understand it either.

She survives by crashing at universities and places where academics hang out. That's where she feels safe. She has made several suicide attempts. I saw her recently and she was very withdrawn. I don't know where she's staying.

Pat

"I came to Vancouver about 25 years ago and landed on the street. I found myself on the street with no place to live, walked into a welfare office—because I had reversed my hours and was up late at night—at quarter to 5. I was told by a woman social worker that the office was closed. I would pick up a man and go home with him, just for a clean bed and sheets, because I had no other alternative and was not aware of the social system, Emergency Services, even if they existed 15 years ago.

"I think people are more aware now of the services available to them, but there are still so many accidents that happen, people that are transient and are not heard.

"I've been really fortunate; I've had men take care of me, feed me, and at a later date they'll walk into a bar and say, 'Is that you?' and I say thank you. I'm not against men; I'm against poverty."

Queen of England

There is one woman on the streets, I call her the Queen of England. She is in her late sixties. One warm and sunny day I saw her; she had on winter boots and sweaters, a hat, a jacket—she was obviously living on the street. I said hi, trying to make conversation, "Where are you staying?" She gave me a chilling look, as only a queen could do, and replied, "Do I know you? Have we met?" I said no, but...She turned her head away, letting me know that further conversation wasn't welcome.

Margaret

"I became homeless in April 1986. I was living with my partner and when the relationship soured, I just packed two suitcases and left. I had been going to a single mothers' support group, and I just asked one of the moms if we (my son and I) could stay with her. Because of the crowded conditions, I just moved from house to house, living out of two suitcases and dealing with the emotional upheaval both my son and myself were experiencing. I met a single mom with two kids who asked me if I wanted to be a roomie with her at a women's housing co-op. I said okay and I moved in July 1986. Since then I have moved, but only into another housing co-op."

Wendy

Wendy is a young woman about 24 years old, who is known by all at Carnegie. She is a friendly, lovable person whose mental sickness is under control with medication.

Wendy fell in love with an older man who gave her a ring. They were to be married, so they lived together. She was so happy, showing everyone her ring and talking about when she and Jack would be married. He took off for another province and never came back. She slowly became sicker and sicker, as she waited and he didn't come back. She was in a shelter, then disappeared, leaving her belongings behind.

Mary and Bill saw her on the street. She was spaced out, dirty, and was obviously homeless and off her medication. They took her into their apartment. She had a shower, ate, had another shower, stayed the night. Mary and Bill are Carnegie members. They gave her the love and caring she needed, and next day she was able to go stay with a relative.

Reaching out to someone can sometimes save their life. This is another invisible homeless story that isn't a statistic.

Notes re: Homeless Women in the Downtown Eastside
by Karen Tully

At the Downtown Eastside Women's Centre, we hear about homelessness every day. The problem seems to have gotten worse for women in the last few years, with rising rental costs and very little protection for tenants. We see a significant number of mothers who are homeless. There are very few places left in Vancouver where single mothers on GAIN can afford to live. Many end up living in small hotel rooms in the downtown eastside because it is the only place they can afford.

Many single mothers are turned away even when they can afford the rent. A woman who uses the women's centre regularly lived for three months with two teenaged children in a small hotel room while searching for an apartment. She went out looking every day. Nine times out of ten, she was told that the building was ADULTS ONLY. Other times she was told that the suite was already rented when they found out she was on GAIN.

We get food donated to the centre by the food bank when they have too much. Usually it is items like bread and fruit. One day I walked up to a woman in the centre and offered her a loaf of bread to take home with her. She laughed bitterly and said, "Yeah right. If I had a home."

"You don't have anywhere to stay?" I asked.

"Sure," she said, "on the street. There's a whole bunch of us. The cops don't know we're there. I come in here to warm up."

Another day. A native woman about 65 years old wants to know if I can call the Old Age Pension office for her and find out why she hasn't been getting her cheques.

"Where are you staying?" I ask her so I can check and make sure the government office has her correct address.

"I don't know. Nowhere," she says.

"You don't have a place to stay?"

"I was staying with my daughter, but they kicked me out."

"Who kicked you out?"

"Her boyfriend. He's a murderer. I'm not staying with him anyway."

We had a woman. I called her Sarah. That wasn't her real name. She's about 50ish. She lived for a while in our back alley, in a shack she had made out of discarded cardboard boxes that she had leaned up against the brick wall on one side of the alley. She lived there all summer and through the fall and winter. I was always worried that a truck or taxi would veer too closely to the left one day and smash down her house, taking her with it. We serve free soup and bannock twice a week at the centre. We used to take her out a bowl of soup. Sometimes she would take it. Sometimes she'd say, "No thanks. I already ate."

I don't know how she stayed warm and dry when the rain started. One day we looked out back and she was gone. We later heard that she had moved to a different alley.

There's a woman, I'll call her Nicky. She lives in her truck. I don't know how long she's been living there, but it's been a while. She moves it to a different parking spot every so often. She comes in to the women's centre for soup and coffee. I asked her why she lives in her truck. She laughed and said, "Have you seen the size of the hotel rooms around here? They're not much bigger than my truck. Anyhow, this way I don't have to deal with landlords or men bothering me. And there's no cockroaches in my truck."

Every week we have women come to us for help to get into a transition house, or short-term emergency shelter like Powell Place or Lookout. Many times, when we call up, we are told that there are no more beds left. We are told to check in again tomorrow to see if any openings have come up. In the meantime, we have nowhere to send a shelterless woman.

Betty McPhee, Crabtree Corners

A couple of days before cheque day, I went to Crabtree Corners Drop-In and Daycare. The place was packed. Women and children were sitting around waiting for the soup to be ready. It smelled good and it was free. Conversation got around to prostitution. One woman said her rent was $500 and if it went up she'd have to work the streets. Some women were going back to work the streets because of rent increases that took all their cheque.

Betty McPhee, who works at Crabtree, said the homeless numbers had increased since I was there a few weeks before. Women were sleeping on the couches in the daytime and walking the streets at night. (At First United Church I saw people asleep on couches too.)

"In the last three years we have seen a big increase. There's a lot more women and children that have moved into the area simply because they have been squeezed out of affordable housing in the rest of Vancouver.

"More and more women are living in violent situations. The transition houses are always backed up. We have women who are living in really crummy hotels that don't have proper locks on the doors. It's a real challenge for the women and kids to get to the bathrooms down the end of the halls in the hotels safely. A couple of instances where women have been raped because a landlord refused to put a decent lock on the goddamn door. There are women sleeping here in the daytime, simply because there is no place for them to go and they're homeless.

"We have women who will go down to Crab Park and stay there, hang out in bars, sometimes turn tricks to get a hotel room. They go to Crosswalk at 12 o'clock if they can get in there at night, but they have to be out early, early in the morning before any of the services are open. These women are extremely vulnerable. A lot of the women use our showers in the morning. They come here for breakfast [after being on the street all night] and of course they come here for lunch, as they do at the women's centre.

"I think the homeless are still fairly invisible, but it's going to become more visible soon. I think we have to save some of the rental stock—all those rooming houses that are being destroyed and there's no replacement. Social housing has to be seen as a priority, and that has to be put into place now. If they don't pay proper attention to the trends and start to do something about it now, and see it as a priority and as a crisis... It can't wait till we get into a situation like San Francisco, where it's so badly backed up.

"Recently we had a couple of visits—one from a journalist from Norway; the other was the wife of an MP in Sweden. The woman had been doing a tour—she was very interested in women's centres in the States—and she was absolutely appalled in Washington, D.C., where people were literally lying on the sidewalks and you had to walk over them, and again in San Francisco, New York, and other large cities. She made an interesting comment that she thought that information was really being repressed, that the image is not getting out into the rest of Europe as to the degree of the homelessness in North America, and it's increasingly looking like, on the streets that is, like a third world country. Somehow we perpetuate the image that everything's alright, and market rents will take care of everything, which is bullshit."

Women's Housing Manifesto

Developed by the Housing Committee of the National Action Committee on the Status of Women, July 1987

1. Adequate, secure, and affordable housing must be recognized as a basic right under the Canadian Charter of Rights and Freedoms. The provision of housing is ultimately a public responsibility.

2. Women are particularly disadvantaged in the housing market because of their lower incomes and because of their responsibility for children. Particular attention should therefore be given to income adequacy and to the provision of affordable and suitable housing for low-income single women and single mothers.

3. Housing should be universally accessible. (Common barriers for women are both physical and social; the latter include household composition, presence of children, source of income, language.)

4. A sufficient number of publicly supported shelters should be provided in every community, with no time limit on stays, for

THE WOMEN

women who are victims of violence, for women who are discharged from institutions, and for women who are otherwise homeless.

5. Shelter alone is not housing; therefore, sufficient and adequate long-term housing must be a priority in every community.

6. Support services must be accessible to women where they live to meet their everyday needs, as well as crises. Security of tenure should not be tied to the need for services.

7. All possible steps should be taken to preserve and maximize use of the existing affordable housing stock; funds should be available for conversion of rental housing to co-operative and nonprofit tenure.

8. Housing policies and programs should recognize the increasing number of nontraditional family forms and provide for their needs. Steps should be taken to promote alternative tenure arrangements for women; low-cost financing should be made available for a range of tenure possibilities; funds for co-ops and nonprofit housing development should be increased.

9. Access to child care and neighbourhood services should be recognized as a fundamental component of any new housing development and established neighbourhood.

10. Women should be involved in the design and delivery of housing, neighbourhoods, and community services, as well as in the management of rental housing.

March

Karen O'Shannacery, Lookout

I am interviewing people who give services to the homeless. I talked to Karen O'Shannacery who works at Lookout, an agency that provides housing and shelter support for the hard to house on an emergency basis. She defines the homeless as "people who are living on the street, or people that are living in emergency accommodation, that have a bed for a few nights here and there." Karen was really adamant that there is a serious accommodation problem in Vancouver.

"Going back one year, our average occupancy rate was 85 percent. It means last year we dealt with something like 1900 people. It means that, out of the 42 beds, there were some available for people. Generally, what was happening last year was, at the beginning of the month you'd have your vacancies during the week, and as you got to the weekend you'd be plugged up, and as you got to cheque issue day your beds would be full again.

"What's happening now is that the beds are full 100 percent of the time. It doesn't matter if it's the day after cheque issue day, the beds are still 100 percent full and we are still turning people away. We're documenting it now—it's something that's brand new because it was never anything that was statistically interesting. A few people turned away and any time we turned someone away, we'd try to get them into some other shelter.

"Affordable housing stock does not exist in the city. People who are on social assistance or any kind of fixed income, if they're trying to get into market rent, they have to pay such an incredible amount of their income, they don't have the money to be able to eat. You can rent a hotel room, *if* you can find one that's vacant. You're talking about a room that's smaller than my office (10 feet by 12 feet), a sink, a window that opens onto a light well that doesn't really give adequate air circulation. It's an older building, most of them have bugs in them, some of them have mice (we have a couple of people who keep the mice as pets), most of them have a bar. This area has more bars in it than anywhere else in the city. And the upkeep of the building is often not done very well.

"The majority of people we see are special needs people. Their needs are not being addressed because of inappropriate housing. The pressure is on even in the hotels because people are moving into the community because this is the affordable place. If there is a family in a hotel, they don't want to put up with someone who might be disruptive, so special needs people get evicted.

"We try to get them into places, try to get Emergency Services to get them a room. But the majority of them are on the street. They crash in cars, garbage cans, at the CBC air vents, underneath the bridges, Stanley Park, everywhere. They say homeless are invisible because if you go to Stanley Park you are not going to see people crashing, but if you are seen you will be evicted. Of course they are not going to be obvious. One of our janitors who knows the area extremely well passes a hotel that's closed. He says there are forty to fifty people, mostly kids, squatting there.

"This is a frustrating problem, and very complex, and it affects people in very complex ways. It's based on two issues: the availability of *affordable* housing—and I put my stress on affordable—and the basic income that people have. You should have some kind of guaranteed income to make sure that everyone can afford a minimum [for rent and food]. It's those two issues, and it's political will that is going to determine whether those two issues are addressed. If you address those two issues, you're going to find that many of the concerns and battles people face on a daily basis—to feed themselves or to get a roof over their heads—those issues will disappear.

"I'll give you an example of some of the battles these people face. Joe came off the streets late at night. He had medical problems. They were not severe enough to need an ambulance. He needed to go to the hospital and get checked out. He had an obvious mental disturbance. He couldn't articulate his needs. It was cold. He didn't have any shoes on. Now we don't have the capability to take someone to hospital, so we rely on the other services. We called Emergency Services for a taxi or bus fare. They said no, his needs were not bad enough. They said we should give him bus fare. Well, we don't have any bus fare. So he didn't go to the hospital. We kept him overnight. Next day we sent him to the clinic. He got agitated because it was crowded and he didn't stay. He just couldn't sit still and wait. He came back to us. He didn't have the ability to address his own needs, and when we tried to give him help to meet his needs, he'd accept our help, but there were no resources out there to help him. He crashed on our couch for three nights, then disappeared. He could be homeless on the street now.

"In this wonderful city of milk and honey there is racism. We had a black woman staying here. She was functioning and all she needed was a home. It took three months to find her one.

"Native people don't have a hope of getting a place outside of the downtown eastside. There's so much of that 'not in my neighbourhood' stuff. You move into a place with your garbage bags and people look down on you, you're stigmatized. And if you isolate people that way, then they're not going to make it. You don't want to isolate people; you don't want to put one woman, for example, in a hotel that's full of just men, because that woman is going to be incredibly victimized, and there's a lot of victimization.

"Often [women] are brought in by a man. They are 'looked after' by men until they are sick enough that they are no longer able to look after them. The women by and large are in worse shape than the men are.

"I hate to admit it but, twenty-four percent of the people we turn away are women. Twenty-one women ended up on the street in January. If we can't find anywhere else for them, we send them to Crosswalk. It only has space for ten people. It opens at midnight. You sit up in chairs, drink coffee. It's safe, but most people don't want to be there. Remember this is only after we phoned Emergency Services to try and get assistance, and other hostel services, when our couches are full. For crying out loud—three couches! This was in January. It was cold. There's no question about it; they will use their bodies to get a roof over their heads.

"There's two things that could be done immediately. One is, the provincial government and the federal government both could give an immediate increase in the number of housing units they're willing to allocate. The federal government has decreased the amount of money they are going to put into social housing stock. The province, by and large, doesn't put much money in. As well, they've been getting rid of illegal suites. The illegal suites are the affordable suites. People are displaced, evicted. They in turn displace the people with special needs.

"One thing governments are doing, that complicates the issue, is, they're saying, we'll give you, for example, the mental health plan—the bright light on the horizon. They're going to give $20 million over the next four or five years to increase community psychiatric support. It doesn't include money for community homes and beds. Hospital beds, yes, licensed facilities, yes, which are mini-institutions. It's not supportive housing, not affordable housing, nothing like that. They've put such restrictions, such government rules on what you can do, and the size of the room, and the staffing, and the kinds of staff you have to have, and the programming, the medication regime, that it really precludes almost anyone from going in and providing some care.

"The other thing that could be done is—we want to get another emergency centre because of the overload. And this is the first time Lookout's agreed to that, because emergency centres, while necessary, are just a band-aid solution. Now, our shelter here was built under the Canadian Mortgage and Housing Corporation's old '56.1' [guideline]. Under that, you had to put aside an amount of money, a reserve, every single year, to be able to deal if the roof comes off or whatever. So we went to CMHC and said, can we use the money we have in the bank as collateral? Because we've got a financial institution that's willing to loan us the money. CMHC said no. A simple policy change by CMHC would have enabled us to start the process to get another emergency shelter.

"It's our own Canadian brand of homelessness. In the States you can't get income, you can't get anything. Here you've got the opportunity but it's inadequate. The pressure is on from the government to let the private sector deal with everything, the community and social problems, and it doesn't happen. The U.S. proves that doesn't happen. But I can see us going down the road to the American way of homelessness. There's no question in my mind—we're going to have people die on the streets."

John Turvey,
Downtown Eastside Youth Activities Society

I went to interview the street nurses, who have a small office off Main. They give out free condoms, they counsel, they give medical information about venereal diseases and AIDS. They work mostly with street people, the homeless. There's a needle exchange program next door that's to help stop drug users from sharing needles that could be contaminated. Street counsellors work in the back of the office.

I sat there for an hour waiting to talk to the nurses. I was so impressed by the respect and kindness that these workers showed to people who needed their services. It wasn't like a welfare office or a medical bureau. You could see that the people that came through the doors were coming into a safe, non-threatening environment. I sat facing the door with a cartoon of a huge condom. There was information on AIDS in an easy-to-read comic and there was other medical literature, all relevant to the street.

This is the community of the homeless who have special housing needs that are not being met, needs that are not even considered according to John Turvey, a Downtown Eastside Youth Activities Society (DEYAS) street worker. Many of the people he works with are children who stay on the street because they don't want to go back to a group home, foster home, or home, period. They survive by exchanging sex for a place to sleep and some drugs to hide the pain.

I have known John Turvey for many years. The first time I met him was about ten years ago. I wanted to do some volunteer work with him, because street work had been my work in Montreal. He interviewed me and said, "We don't need another fucking honky" (and him as white as a piece of paper).

I respect his work. He's always been there, working at street level. He has been called the "coach"; not for sports, but because of the number of street kids who, when pregnant, asked him to coach their births.

"You're now seeing people asking for more co-op housing. Well, co-op housing means nothing but the fucking middle class. It gentrifies the neighbourhood. It's got nothing to do with our client group down here.

"We've got mental health casualties. We've got a lot more women in the area that are at risk. We've got children that are at risk. We've got intravenous drug users that are at risk. We've got subcultural groups of street people, like the transsexuals that get thrown out of the women's centre. They basically are homeless but nobody'll call them that, and that's within our own community—the great, enlightened downtown eastside. And most of that population's been here a long time.

"All of a sudden some people claim some moral high ground and so they're out. They weren't given any notice, there wasn't any planning for their eviction, they were just out. So those people stay up all night and that's the new homeless. They drink to go to sleep, they sleep in the street, or they sleep in the daytime in social services offices or in the court house or wherever they can. They do everything that people that don't have a home do. They sleep at other people's places, they sleep here, they sleep there, they stay up all night, they sit up in restaurants—they do all that shit, sell themselves, whatever.

"I don't see that our community has really shared the expertise—like the housing groups, like DERA and First [United] Church, aren't coming out to specialized resources like our group, to teach us how to do housing. And yet they refuse to service our people.

"All the politically correct agencies are not going to house the intravenous drug users, they're not going to house HIV positive street people. They'll be up at City Hall claiming to represent the homeless... but the homeless we work with? They don't represent them! They won't even let them in the compounds they call housing. They're not going to accommodate the poorly educated, non-white, minority person with special needs—they're not nice enough, and they don't know how to 'do it' properly. Well, granted, they don't. Why the fuck aren't we teaching them? Why aren't we building housing that's appropriate for these people?

"Housing could be renovating the places that are already there, taking ownership. It could be small, it could be large. We don't even know because nobody's taking the risk.

"So we're going to do housing for HIV positive street people, right. We're just going to fucking do it, and the community can go to hell in a handbasket as far as I'm concerned. I find the community's putting these people out to dry, just like the mainstream culture. We're going to do it now, we're getting a few thousand bucks from the federation for immune diseases. We're going to start our own fucking housing. We'll just do it."

Homelessness has many faces, many different needs; there are not enough resources of the right kind. When governments give money to some groups, and others with equal need are left out, the danger is debilitation. Instead of unity it creates powerlessness. That's what the Haves want: the Have-nots fighting over peanuts.

It is easier to house people that are together, so easy to overlook the multiple problems. Co-ops are forced by government regulations to charge market rents for some housing to balance subsidised housing, which of course means less housing for people on welfare and other pensions. People and families are entitled to safe, clean, reasonable housing at low cost, but the problem is that there is not enough money, not enough law, not enough protection by government of safe reasonable housing for all who need it. The marketplace does not protect us from rental abuse. We have no protection at the moment, no rentalsman. The community at large must fight this. Where are the mentally sick and the drug users and the people with AIDS to live? If they are to get well, don't they need a home too? Do they have a choice when they live on the street?

DERA undertook a survey of 130 downtown eastside hotels and rooming houses, and interviewed 100 tenants, in February 1990. Some of the findings:

Most downtown eastside residents live well below the poverty line, and rely primarily on welfare/GAIN or other forms of social assistance for their income.

More young people, including more women and children, are moving into the area.

Since 1986 the community has lost 19 hotels (723 units) to demolition, closure, or gentrification, and is facing the loss of another 18 hotels (1014 units).

Applicants to social housing face a one or two year wait list.

There were 42 known shelterless people in January (Urban Core Shelterless Committee).

DERA Housing has a wait list of 2772 applicants, of which

319 are families and 1286 seniors. Of these, 50 families and 448 seniors have listed single room occupancy hotels as their principal residence.
DERA Newsletter, *March 1990*

Apartment vacancy rates in B.C

	% Ap/87	% Ap/90
Greater Vancouver	2.4	0.9
Greater Victoria	1.1	0.7
Mission	3.4	0.0
Abbotsford	2.9	0.2
Chilliwack District	5.0	0.1
Penticton	2.2	0.3
Kelowna	0.7	0.1
Vernon	5.6	0.1

figures from Canadian Mortgage and Housing Corp.

The city's social planning department estimates that about 25 percent of Vancouver's residential hotel and rooming-house stock, approximately 3000 units, has been lost in the past 10 years. And a study done for the city by consultants Burgess, Austin and Associates predicts that of the 9000 remaining low-cost rooming-house units in the downtown and eastside areas, about 1600 (17 percent) will be lost to development in the next 10 years.
from "The Homeless" by Moira Farrow, Western Living, *April 1990*

In Metro Toronto in the early 1980s...
- there were at least 3400 people with no permanent address
- 1600 of these people were in hostels; 1800 were clients of social service agencies who were not staying in hostels
- 36 percent of the homeless in hostels were single people under age 25

from No Place to Go, A Study of Homelessness in Metropolitan Toronto: Characteristics, Trends and Potential Solutions, *a study by the Metro Toronto Planning Department*

In 1987 in Quebec...
- public housing units have doubled since 1981
- there are still 45,000 people on waiting lists for these units
    from "Homelessness and the Homeless," by H. Peter Oberlander and Arthur L. Fallick

April

The Vancouver and District Public Housing Tenants Association held their annual meeting on April 4, 1990. About 100 people who live in public housing attended. In her report, Margaret Mitchell, the president of the Association, said that government policies are increasing poverty. She listed some of the problems poor people face:
- Seniors are robbed at every turn by high rents and expensive medicine.
- People who are mentally ill are told to ask for help themselves, but sometimes they can't do this.
- Free trade is pushing our jobs to the U.S. The jobs of U.S. workers are going to Mexico because of low wages. Mitchell said we must not resort to attacking people because of their background or what country they're from. It's not their fault that they are wanted as exploited labour.
- Housing is being used to make profit, not to provide places for the poor to live. Mitchell said we need more public housing. In B.C. alone, there is a need for 125,000 units of public housing.

Margaret Mitchell defines homelessness as having to face the private market without income. The private market does not service the poor.

I went back to see the street nurses again. There is always a line-up for free condoms, counselling. When it's time for my interview, I usually get bumped because a street person is in crisis. I wait patiently because I know the street nurses' customers take priority. I figure it must look as if this grandmother uses a hell of a lot of condoms. I have been spending quite a bit of time outside the nurses' door, waiting, thinking about what I've been hearing.

The door of the needle exchange at the street nurses' office

One of the problems or confusions I'm facing is that some people say there is a homeless problem and others say it's not too bad yet. It's not as bad as the problem in the States. They say, "You can see the homeless in the States, you trip over them. It's not like that here." Agencies are trying to count the homeless, but in my opinion that count gives us an incorrect figure. You can't count the people sleeping in Stanley Park and other parks and out of the way places homeless people hide. They often don't want to be found because they can be told to move on or get out. If I were homeless I wouldn't sleep where I could be found.

I am increasingly aware that there is not enough preparation being done by government agencies to prevent a serious homeless situation like the one in the States. Instead, it's being hushed over, as if, if we ignore it, it will go away.

Alan Alvare, First United Church

"Any time the weather turns cold, in come the requests for sleeping bags and heavy blankets. Some of the requests come from people living in places with broken or token heating arrangements. Some come from people living outside. What strikes me is the resourcefulness of people in finding the 'best' outdoor locations. It reminds me of films about Rio and Manila, where people compete for the best cardboard boxes. What also strikes me is the casual way real estate is talked about in newspapers, sometimes the same newspapers that people use to insulate their clothes or shoes. There's something so radically wrong here that even parroting biblical references to this kind of injustice is likely to take the edge off it.

"Welfare gives people $275 for rent. And if you believe places are available for that, have I got a bridge for you! The pressure on downtown hotel accommodation has increased as more refugees from rent-hiked apartments move into the Downtown Eastside. People spend their food money, go hungry, and then get blamed for having no energy to 'organize' or 'plan' their lives.

"Another easy-to-blame group are discharged mental patients. Even some downtown hotels are reluctant to take this population.

"Every day at least one person spends a few hours sleeping in a pew or on one of the sofas in the hall. Usually they're people who look like they've been outside for long periods of time. We don't disturb them."

I ask myself, how can a single person, between 19 and 65 years old, rent accommodation for the $275 per month that welfare allows for rent, hydro, and phone? How? Minimum wage isn't enough to rent an apartment, is it?

My frustration rises as I talk to a young woman with a serious disability that's permanent. She isn't yet on a handicap allowance. She wants to leave an abusive relationship. Her rent allowance is $275. She tried to find a place to live, but couldn't find anything under $400. She ended up going back to the abuser. She was crying, upset. She had tried to kill herself two weeks before. She is only 26 years old. She tried to go to a shelter but when she mentioned she was on medication, they told her she would have to be under observation for 24 hours. She was frightened and went away, went back to an abusive relationship.

End Legislated Poverty had its annual general meeting. There were groups there from all over the province, and we had to pick which issue was the biggest priority. Housing took precedence.

One woman from the North Shore told of problems native people were having, being discriminated against. She told of people sleeping outside in the rain and cold this winter.

Families have problems finding housing in Nelson. You can get a bachelor suite, but that's about it.

When we finished the meeting, it was agreed that there is a serious shelter problem, that rental controls must return, and that welfare and minimum wage must be raised, or more and more people will be on the street.

Stephen Learey, DERA

I went to interview Stephen Learey who works for DERA. He was upset. A hotel in the community was evicting 60 tenants. City Hall had ordered the owners to do repairs that were needed, but the owners refused and were threatening to close the hotel.

"A lot of hotels are being cracked down on for their conditions. There's now a lot of discussion on what shall we do about this?

We can't let hotel conditions deteriorate. We can't say we're going to ease up on the by-laws. There are people in the community advocating that forcing hotels to clean up is evicting people, and we shouldn't force hotels to clean up. But right now we have ten problem hotels out of 380 in this community. If we lower the standards then we'll have 380 problem hotels instead of ten.

"People are moving out of hotels because there are problems with those hotels. If someone can't walk very well and the elevator's not working, and you say, 'Elevators don't really have to be working; we're going to lower the standards,' then you've evicted that person who can't walk very well.

"One thing that really bugs me is people who are in decent housing themselves, saying that the city should lower its criteria for hotels. We have people coming in daily, asking us to call the city to get their hot water on, or their heat on, or their elevator working. Yet people in the community, who have decent housing, say we should lower the level. The day the people who live in the hotels say lower the level, that's when we will listen. We take our guidance from the people who are affected.

"There's obviously some basic levels we'd like to see. Each inspector seems to have a different level and I know hotels they're looking very closely at when there's other hotels that seem to be in much worse shape. I think they could tighten that up a little bit.

"I think that shutting down a hotel should be the ultimate last. The city has to be more involved in fixing up that housing and charging it to the owner. They did it once, but they seem reluctant to do it again. They say it's going to cost too much. But each 20 or 50 unit hotel they shut down, our problems get worse and worse and worse. Once these hotels are shut, they very seldom open up again. Once they're shut, we lose that housing. There were hotels on Granville that were torn down and turned into commercial buildings, theatres.

"What's happening is a government plan and a city plan to make this a world class city, to bring money in from around the world. We invited international money. Everyone wants a piece of the city now. All of a sudden a guy who owns a crummy little hotel, say fifty units, rooms that rent for $250 to $300 a month, realtors come by and ask, do you want to sell the place? He says, how much? out of curiosity, and he gets offered a million and a half dollars for his building. What's he going to do? We get calls from hotels often, asking us if we want to buy because they know we build social housing.

"It's land speculation. The price of land has increased to such a point that every piece of land looks interesting. We are going to have luxury condos costing a quarter of a million. Who the hell can afford that? The super rich. They have to spend their money somewhere, so all of a sudden around where these places are built, places start popping up to cater to them. All these designer clothes shops, right in the downtown eastside, because there's this new group of people who will only buy at those places. All the land around these big projects, people start looking at them.

"Along Pender where the old Expo site was, there are five [low-rental] hotels and a detox centre across the street from where they are going to build three luxury towers, one of them being a hotel and two of them luxury condos. Something's going to go. Within a one block radius of that development at Pender and Abbott, there are a thousand people living in hotel rooms. One thousand people. So of course that block is going to come down, as other developers say, 'Maybe I'll build a health spa, or maybe a beauty salon, a cosmetic shop'—nothing for us, but for the tourists.

"City hall either has to stop what's happening, or put something in so that, for every unit that's lost, there's another unit

A rally at the Del-Mar Hotel, the "one skinny little hotel" that didn't sell out to downtown Vancouver development

created—and that's for the same price. So you have a hotel that has fifty units that rent for $300 a month; if a developer wants to use that piece of land, he can do it, but he must replace those units. You've got to put pressure on city hall. [Mayor Gordon Campbell] can do things himself. He has the power to stop what's happening. But he's putting it on to other levels of government.

"We have research from other cities that have this stuff in place. They say, if you want to be a developer, this is what it's going to cost you to be a developer. San Francisco, Seattle have by-laws that recognise that developers have to contribute to society. Like, you don't get to make your millions and walk away and cause all kind of problems. We have a situation in our community with BC Hydro tearing down affordable units. They don't have a development permit yet. Next to Vancouver Vocational Institute there's a big pit, except for one hotel. One skinny little hotel—the Del-Mar—didn't sell out, but everything else has been destroyed. They tore down that housing even though they have no plans to build anything there. When developers can do that and walk away, City Hall is not doing its job."

Street Nurses

I don't believe my luck. Today I actually got a meeting with the street nurses, these very overworked women who are so liked and respected by the community. While I was there, a note was delivered to them. It was a thank-you note in the form of a hand-done cartoon. It had a picture of Tarzan and Jane and it said, "Thanks. Jane don't itch no more and neither does Tarzan."

"What we do is go out on the street, talk to people, talk to kids. Anyone that we think may be able to use our services. At that time also we meet people who don't have a place to stay. At that time we try to make some kind of contact.

"We deal with a wide variety of people, different ages, and we have multiple problems as far as housing goes. What I see here is young people that are in care, have left their group homes, are living on the street, maybe associating with a restaurant. Maybe they get a room for the night because they wash dishes. They don't want to go back to the group homes. Then we have people who are perhaps mentally ill, who are not stabilized anymore, not taking their medication, have nowhere to go, need emergency housing for the night. That might be either Triage or Lookout."

"We have had people that we weren't able to house. What's happened in these cases, we contact their worker to get a room in a hotel for the night. It's not the best, basically just a room with a bed, a wash basin if they're lucky.

"Some people won't go near Social Services. They choose to stay out for many reasons: sometimes they're overcrowded and they don't receive the support and care that they need. And they get a lot more from their peers on the street, a lot more support and that kind of thing.

"There isn't enough [street level service]. I think these are the people who will not go anywhere until they're almost on their hands and knees. If we can get to them before they reach that point it would be more cost effective for the ministry of health, getting to these people before there's a major crisis. It's going to be more costly if they need hospitalization.

"I would prefer, rather than these large institutionalized places, more social housing on a smaller scale, homes that people can feel is their home. Maybe 10 or less people, somewhere around there. I don't think there's a magic number, but somewhere where people have their own place, and feel part of the community, part of that home. Maybe with some supervision depending on their problems.

"Of course these people don't have much of a voice in this society anyway. Frankly a lot of times these people are not even landed immigrants. They're not going to express it. We have a lot of Spanish-speaking people here, people who feel threatened by and very suspicious of any authority. Their voice certainly isn't going to be heard. These people have always been considered the rejects. They're not going to be very vocal and there aren't any town meetings and that kind of thing happening around here."

People sometimes say it's a waste of time, giving housing to drug users, substance abusers, etc. They say they don't deserve it. Do you have a success story?

"I know of one, she's a transsexual. I have known her for approximately eleven years. She's in her early forties. Anyway, I met her in a bar. She's usually very cheerful, takes pride in her appearance. She came up to me, she seemed very obviously distressed. She was ready to do herself in. She had reached her limit. So right away we talked about getting her into a detox. Next morning we got her into a detox outside of town. In the meantime she had seen a doctor, got some tests done. She found out she is HIV positive. This is the virus that causes AIDS. After her treatment she really tried. She had been a user for a good many years. It was very difficult; she had been using drugs since she was fourteen. Heroin, cocaine, she's always been on and off the streets. Then she went into a treatment centre. It's been hard, but she's still holding it together. And been getting support from various people and organizations. She's doing okay. Now she's thinking about getting a job—and people are helping her with that. She's going to NA and AA meetings.

"I feel like she's one of our success stories. However, in the meantime, she's found out that she is HIV positive and that's something else she is going to have to deal with."

You mentioned going into the bar. I don't think it was for a beer, was it?

"We go into the bars to meet people. When we started, we started as more outreach, to get people to come in and see us. Now that we have established ourselves and gained that respect, we have so many people coming in to see us that we hardly get a chance to go out on the street. We have people lining up at the door. You're torn. Should you tell the people at the door to go away so that you can do your street work, or do you stay and see them? This is the dilemma we are facing. Initially we were doing a lot more of that, getting out there and meeting the people in the bars and on the street corners. Just telling them who we are."

Are you scared of the danger?

"I know that some of the people that started here originally have expressed those kind of concerns and you do always have to be careful. But you have to be careful wherever you are. I don't feel threatened. I don't know, maybe because I feel that I've been here for so long, maybe I feel almost like a part of the community. I think people who have had obvious mental disturbances, mental health problems, and have gone off their medication and are paranoid, and whatever, might reach a point where they might lash out. That is probably my greatest fear."

What is your definition of homelessness?

"I guess a person who doesn't have a space, where they feel they can be comfortable, of their own. When people don't have adequate access to running water, bathrooms, toilets, there are lots of people who don't have access to a shower, which means they can't wash... if they have something like scabies, it can be passed on to other people. They can't take care of themselves, so it leads to the spread of disease. It's in society's best interest to take care of these people."

Interview with a Hotel Manager

After I finished tutoring at Carnegie I went to check out the Silver Lodge. This was the hotel that was evicting 60 tenants. I wanted to know where the people were going to go and what were the reasons for the hotel's closing. I knew that community groups were doing all they could to help, and to organize the tenants.

I went up the dark, dirty inside stairs. At the top there was a locked door with a "No Visitors" sign. I knocked with my fist on the door. The man that opened the door was obviously filling in for the manager. He was withdrawn, elderly, looked real sick, and didn't want to talk to me. I asked him if it was true that the hotel was closing. He said, "Yeah, yeah." I asked him, "Are you going to be homeless too? Where are you going?" He shook his head and said, "The manager's asleep, he's asleep." Couldn't find out too much there, so I went back down the stairs out into the sunlight.

I have a friend, David, who runs another hotel nearby, so I went to see him. He knew the owners of the hotel. He knew exactly what was happening and why. I sat in his little office. It had an old stove, an old fridge, a big colour TV, a sink with a faded yellow curtain around it. The window overlooked the stairs so he could see who was out there before he let them in. He stopped talking every time he heard footsteps on the stairs and we would both listen to the clomp, clomp, clomp until the person came in sight of the window. One woman, about forty years of age, a resident, came to the window. Her face was covered in bruises. She smiled hello just as if the bruises were part of her normal face.

I was upset. My stomach turned to knots. I wanted to jump up and ask her, who did this to you? Did you charge them? Did you get medical care? Down here you don't ask too many questions unless you know the person. Or unless they invite questions. After she left, I asked my friend what had happened to her. He said a trick had beat her up the night before.

David had so much information that isn't in the papers or on TV. He is there night and day and he sees it all: suicides, MSSH paying rent for a 17-year-old to live in a skid row hotel, a man found starved to death in the back lane. It's strange how society thinks it is only university people that are experts on poverty and skid row and homelessness, yet this man is an expert, too.

"I live and work in Skid Road. I kind of like the name Skid Road. It's a natural name and it goes back in history because this is where they skidded the logs down and put them on the boats. Carroll and Powell—they used to come down Water Street, or they used to come from the other end, down Powell, and skid the logs down and put them on the boats. You've got to remember the water was right up against Powell Street. That goes back to Gassy Jack's day, about 100 years ago.

"I've been in this hotel for a number of years and the thing is, the fire department to me is a little too strict with some people and not strict enough with others, because there are some hotels in the east end that are definitely falling down. Falling down from the inside out. When you've got a hotel that's 85, 90 years old, they can't make a Hyatt Regency or the Vancouver Hotel out of it. I don't care how much they spend. They have to tear it right down and start over again.

"I heard that the fire marshall took the owners [of the Silver Lodge] to court. They got a fine for things such as the cleaner was cleaning the hallways, and he put the garbage cans at the end of the hallways so that he could finish up and dump the garbage cans and get it all done. Had the fire marshall come an hour later, it would have been all done. They got fined for propping the fire door open while they were mopping the floors.

"Then a building inspector came to see the place. He said, if you don't clean up the hotel we'll do it for you. This came from city hall, and they stated that it would run about a hundred thousand dollars. To do that, they would have to take that hotel and tear it down to the foundation and start over again. So the owners just closed it down.

INTERVIEW WITH A HOTEL MANAGER

"How I see homelessness is... let's start with the younger people on the street. DEYAS can't keep up with them. These people want to be on the street. I would sooner see them all taken off and put in places where they can live, rather than sleeping in parked cars or burned-out vans or something. If they come into this hotel, I have the Kiddy Car number [the branch of the Police Department that looks after the juveniles], and I call the Kiddy Car for them.

"Then there's the age bracket 20 to 40. They should have homes for some of these people too. Just because they can tell the difference between one dollar and two dollars, that don't mean they're safe to walk the streets. They can't look after themselves and they don't realize their rent has to be paid. They're given their money, they spend it, then they have no place to go. That's why they have places like the Lookout that's filled. There should be other places like the Victory House for these people. They should be paying people to look after them. They shouldn't just be turned loose like that.

"I have people in here, I've had people in here, that have come here with a voucher and the minute they do something wrong and I remind them, they say 'I want my money back.' But I can't give them money back, and they can't understand that. And to try to get the worker to understand this... The worker says they must be fit to live out here if they are not put away. I've had 20 year olds who had to have the street nurse come in to clean up their rooms. I've had one girl who came here every second day to give out medication to different people living in the hotel. I see it every day, people out there. I don't care what the health team says, it's there. I see it every day.

"I would sooner give a woman a room than to have the woman say, 'Hey! I went to him, gave him sex just to put a roof over my head.' That's the sad part about that. Oh yes, it happens. It happens quite regular. I've had women come in here and offer me sex for a room. They get tired of sleeping out. They've gone for two days with no place to sleep or they've been over at some place like the Crosswalk where they're put out at 6 in the morning and they're not allowed back in until 2 a.m., and you can't go on with four hours sleep a night. That's what drives these people to drinking so much that they're into the booze. You just get fed up and people can't cope with it.

"I try to check everybody coming in. I don't want people coming in with drugs. That's a no-no. I don't want people coming in that are going to be drunk 24 hours a day, and into the cooking wine and all the rest of that. I don't want them in here because I have a mixed crowd in the hotel. My tenants run anywhere from their late teens to 65 years, I have to be very careful who I bring in. I don't rent to the first person that comes along. I found out that people that usually sleep outside in the summer come into the hotels for the winter. When they come in they show the hotel no respect, so I have to be very careful. I have rules and regulations set up for the tenants in here.

"Another reason I'm very fussy who comes into the hotel, I don't want people with sex crimes. They're the wrong type of people to have in the hotel. I don't care if it's in the east end, the west end, the north end—there should be places set up for them to live in.

"I know some success stories, two women that I helped both have jobs in stores. I remember when they came here, they had totally nothing but a voucher from welfare for a room. Both these women are doing fine now. The only way I helped them, I made sure they had breakfast in the morning, and when they came home at night I always made sure there was something. I always keep macaroni and some kind of meat—hamburger meat or bacon. [He showed me a fridge that he keeps in his office, a big old fridge. He buys food and keeps it in there to help people out.] In this day and age I can't see why anybody can stand by and see someone hungry, especially if the other person's fighting to get ahead. I can't help everybody in the city out, but those that I can, I will. There are teenagers living in the hotel now and that's one thing they'll verify to, that I make sure I knock on their door and ask them if they've eaten. One girl goes out and panhandles. One is just turned 17, and one has just turned 19. Welfare's paying for them to stay here in Skid Road.

"This is something I can't figure out, why these people, why don't they put them in North Vancouver, Shaughnessy, why not up there? Well, the people wouldn't tolerate it. They tell these kids, you go out and get a room. They don't question where it is. You get a room and show me proof that you have a room reserved for you and we'll give you a cheque or make out a voucher to the people there. If welfare does that, these kids are gonna end up here. This is the cheapest rent. We charge $220. Our rent has not gone up since way before Expo.

"When you talk about Skid Road, I can understand when they say 'these slum lords.' Any man that charges $275 for a room with a sink and a bed and a dresser, that is approximately 12 feet by 15 feet—$275 per person—that man should be taken out, or forced to live in that room, given the same amount as that person on welfare. I don't care if he owns the hotel. I know the owner of this hotel; he phones first thing in the morning and last thing at night. In the other hotels it can go on for months. The owner comes round once a month and picks the cheques and money up, and once he's got that, he's gone again, and you don't see him for 30 days, you don't hear from him.

"At one point I had a bootlegger behind me in a hotel, peddling out the back door. It was like a junky's haven on one side of me, and on the other side of me there was a whore house. This kind of made me laugh because people are saying 'Make sure you run a clean hotel.' I know what I'm doing, I know this business. But why don't they go to these other places? Last month the manager of one hotel was caught selling coke. He was caught by the police and he had enough gall to phone up here and ask if I had a room for him. This fellow was selling to the tenants—he was selling to his own tenants. And this way, nobody on the street is gonna know about it. I sat and watched him shoot up, shooting it in their arms, in the windows of the hotel next to me. The tenants in my hotel came down and complained.

"If they [tenants] are mentally ill and really incapable of helping themselves, they can be taken advantage of so easy. I have two in here right now that I have to truly keep my eye on, to make sure no one takes advantage of them and to make sure they're alright because they have no other place to go. I have a couple of alcoholics in here. When they're flush and they've got money and they get loaded, they sleep with their door open. They go and crash and leave their door open. I gotta go around and make sure all the doors are closed. I don't want some guy getting robbed. These people are not just tenants, they're friends. I can go down Skid Road and some of these people sleeping in alleys are friends of mine. They're sleeping in alleys because they have no other place to go. Nobody will take them.

"My definition of homelessness is a person that is on the street, one that is living under a viaduct or something. Not only living there, but a person who has no friends. I still think in this day and age a friend will help another friend out.

"I have it here in the hotel, friends try and sneak people in here. 'It's my brother.' Well, I know it's not his brother and it's not his sister and it can't be his mother, because she's only a year younger than him. Some of these people got the largest families you've ever run into. Everybody they bring in is either a sister, brother, mother, their uncle, aunt. One guy had seven fathers, according to him. He would bring them in and try to put them up in his room overnight. I had to put a stop to him; he was bringing them in four or five a night. I could turn my back once in a while, but when it comes to four or five, and then it would be seven nights a week like that.

"It's definitely gonna get worse before it gets better. It's gotta get worse. The city is making sure these hotels are closed up and everybody is a slum landlord. Well everybody *isn't* a slum landlord who operates a hotel. There are some hotels that have to be closed, grant you. They'll end up on the street, sleeping in cardboard boxes or under the viaduct or something. As a matter of fact, I have a fellow here who slept under the viaduct because he said the hotels he was staying in were falling down around him. He said, 'Under the viaduct I'm not plagued with cockroaches. I don't have to go to bed with cotton batten in my ears.' And he came to this hotel and he's still here. He says I spoil him. That's exactly what he said.

"As a matter of fact, I can walk out of here and lock this office door and stay out all day. If anything goes wrong, the tenants will take care of it themselves. If the wrong person walks in, the tenants will put him out. I have had one tenant here six years, and this man has laid down another layer of plywood. He took the time to paint his own room, bone white. He painted the floor. He took two-by-fours and four-by-fours and he made his own bed. The only thing he has in that room that belongs to us, other than the sink, is the sheets and the blankets and the mattress. He's lived here for six years and he says he'll die here if they don't tear the hotel down before he does.

"If I wrote a book on the things I've seen happen in this hotel, people would say it's a lie, it's fiction. I've seen people come in here right off the street, with jeans and a T-shirt and a summer jacket in the winter. Within a year they've had a job, they've moved into a basement suite or an apartment. They cleaned up their act 100 percent. And I've seen other people come in here with some idea—they come up from Ontario or Quebec—that, 'I hope Vancouver's waiting for me.' You should hear them say this. In the meantime, Vancouver's been here 100 years or more, and it hasn't been waiting for that particular person to come up here. I've seen them go right downhill—I've seen them go down and end up sitting in front of that all-night restaurant. That place shouldn't have closed up. If the police closed it, then all those people gonna go somewhere else. Then we gotta worry where they're gonna be next.

"We've had one suicide here. A man came all the way from the east coast, it took him 18 years to get here because he was in and out of jail all along the way. When he went up to see his sister she called him a drunk. He went in his room and took pills, washed them down with the wine and got out the Bible. And that's how we found him.

"One person was found in an alley just around the corner a couple of years ago. His stomach was totally empty of food; he had not eaten for a day or two. There was no alcohol in his system. The police said he just went in there and died. This was a man 45 years old. He was just a body. Never did hear what his name was and I don't know if anyone ever found out. That's wrong, at 45 you should be just starting to live. Not just crawl up in an alleyway and call it quits. They do give out food here, but lots of people don't realize it.

"When people got that letter last year from the welfare office saying get a job or you're cut off your cheque, there were two suicides from that. One was in the hotel we were just discussing, and the other was in a hotel over on Cordova Street.

"One fellow had just come out of a mental institution and he was told that his welfare would be cut if he did not get a job or have proof he was looking for a job. Two days before he was supposed to report to welfare, he went in his room and hung himself. It wasn't in the paper either. The one on Cordova was printed in the paper just 'man died suddenly.' The one on Cordova couldn't make it on the money he had, so he got fed up with everything. He couldn't pay his rent. Rather than be kicked out because he couldn't pay the rent and survive too, he called it quits. I forget whether he used a rope or a towel around his neck.

"I'll be honest with you: this last year I've seen the police treating the homeless a lot different, 100 percent better. Up to approximately a year ago they did not seem to care; they would just put them in the wagon, take them to detox. I found a woman and a man sleeping in the washrooms in this hotel. They had come up through the fire exit, no place to sleep, and they sat in the men's washroom, and no one could get into the washrooms because they were sleeping. The woman weighed about 90 pounds, the fella about 125 pounds. That police officer picked that woman up so gentle you would have thought it was his child, she was that small. He picked her up and carried her out in his arms. I don't even think she woke up. I watched him put her gently in the wagon. They had been drinking.

"Every day I see homeless people. City hall might say there's not a homeless problem; they're the only ones who can't see the problems of the city. I honestly believe from the bottom of my heart that God Campbell is trying to move the people out of the east end. The property down here is worth a lot of money and, as you know, city hall is for the unholy dollar. They don't care who they hurt to get it. When a man can stand by and watch a house come down, knowing six families are going to be out on the street, and he says that's progress—and that's exactly what he said. I watched him say it on TV and never forgot it.

"God Campbell and his disciples sit up in city hall and they dictate to the people what they are going to do, and people have to accept it. It's that simple.

"As far as where they're going to go, that's a tough decision. I don't know who's going to make that decision, but there's going to be no place to go around here. I think that's why they're opening up Surrey the way they are; they say it's just to take a bit of the overload from here. But the thing is, when they tear down a hotel, say it's 60, 70, 80 years old, they put up a concrete building. That building is there to stay for 100 years, 150 years. It's either an office building or something that is no help to these people. It helps someone with a business, that's it.

"I think the city wants the property all around here. I honestly do. It's that simple. God Campbell and his disciples are taking care of all of their friends, and the premier, when he tried to give away the Expo site for a few dollars to his friend and he said all we are is friends. Friendship goes a long way when it comes to the unholy dollar. Marketplace! Does it take care of people in the rental market? Do you belive that? In a pig's ass! Name one cent Vander Zalm's ever given you."

The Squatters

A friend called and told me about some young people who were squatting in some vacant houses on Frances Street in the east end. The houses had been sold for development but demolition hadn't started. I decided to go and look for the squatters. I don't know too much about squatting, but it sure sounds better than sleeping on the street.

I knocked on the door where the windows had no drapes. The door was nailed up. Obviously I wasn't going to get an answer, so I went around to the back. Still nothing.

A young man came out of the garage; it looked like he had been sleeping there. I said "Hi, I'm looking for the squatters."

"There's nobody here," he said, not trusting me. Why should he? I was someone he didn't know. I told him about my book and who I was, and that I wanted to interview the people who were squatting. He went over to the back of the next house. I sat on the stone steps leading to the basement of the first house. A couple of young men and a woman came out. I explained again who I was and what I wanted to do, desperately wanting them to know I wasn't an enemy.

I was lucky. Another young man came over from the third house. He said he had heard me read poetry on Co-op Radio. The others were reluctant, but agreed to talk on my little tape deck. Other people came and went. I introduced myself to them as they arrived. Some had been homeless, living on the street. Others had been evicted. Some had been staying with friends. There were people of colour, white people, all different ages, different backgrounds. They were organized, articulate, polite, and had a great sense of community. They had pulled down the fences that separated the homes so they could share. The yards had discarded toys, left by the children of former tenants who had had to leave. Last year's flowers and this year's weeds grew together. The people's identities and their shadows were still there; I wonder where they went, these tenants that had had to move because the marketplace was so greedy.

I was pleased that these young people were organizing and fighting back against developers, and a government that is not protecting its people.

"There are four houses that are definitely squatted, and we've had help from two of the tenanted houses which are also slated for demolition. It's a row of six houses which are going to become condominiums.

"I found out about some of the former tenants. My house was empty for five months before I got here. It's in excellent condition. Two houses down, the tenants were a family living there for eight years. Their landlord was very unscrupulous, didn't tell them at all until he had completed the deal with Ning Yee the developer. All of a sudden they had two months notice to get out. The next door neighbour had been living there for twelve years and all along the landowner had been saying, 'I'm never planning to sell. I'm never planning to sell,' and the tenants put a lot of money into renovation. All of a sudden they got two months notice to vacate.

"I got here two months ago. The houses filled up very quickly after that. There's about fifteen people over four houses."

"One of the houses on the block, there was a gentleman living in the house for twenty years by himself, then they gave him notice and he's got two months only to move and find a place. It disrupted his life, I bet, without compensation of any type.

"We got a week's notice from the landlord to get out; a threat that if we were not out in one week he would call the police. We responded by first designing and posting posters—about homelessness and gentrification, and about emergency procedures, what to do—inviting people who lack housing to move into surplus housing that's not being used, and issuing press statements."

"There's been a lot of media coverage splashed all over the place; the way it has been presented is this very desperate response, because of displacement and gentrification. That's the angle it's gone, but...but they missed the positive side of squatting. In many ways, it's preferable to renting. For me, this is the first time I've ever felt part of a community, not just a scene. There's a lot of solidarity because you're all in it together, and a lot more need for co-operation, and because you're so close you obviously get to know each other a lot better. People tore down all the fences—that was one of the first things that happened. It was very small but very symbolic.

"I don't think there's the same sort of hopelessness with us as in the downtown eastside. A lot of people that are squatting here have come from fairly desperate conditions. Some people had been selling their food because they couldn't afford rents and stuff like that. I don't get the same feeling; I think there's a difference between the downtown eastside and the squatting in the east side, if you know what I mean. We all came in here and all of us wanted to live here and to make a political statement. We were all, right from the start, organizing around that.

"People are getting the impression that we are only students here, young, youth, single, what have you. It's not the case. There's a woman that has two children and she's pregnant. She needs a place to live and it's very difficult for her to find a place. She's on fixed income. We've got houses with electricity and other utilities. There's no reason why we should give this up to sleep in an alley.

"I see squatting as a much more viable response than lobbying the government. People are doing it themselves and they're not depending on the benevolence of someone who has power to help them. They're empowering themselves."

"It should really be noted the amount of positive community support we've been getting. Everyone has their own eviction story or their rent being raised, so there's been a lot of support for these squats. Gentrification is at the level where people can't just keep moving further east."

"Gentrification is like what's happening in New York, U.S., Europe, inner cities, where you have a concentration of poor people and quite often they're visible minorities. The governments leave these places to be derelict. As far as crime is concerned, they turn a blind eye. Then landlords don't repair, like slumlords.

Then you get evictions, and they put in hotels, high-priced playgrounds for the rich, adult-oriented housing.

"The people from wealthier neighbourhoods are being affected too, and they are moving east. They're being evicted and they're moving east, and that in turn is moving the people from the east into the downtown eastside which is in turn pushing up the rents in the hotels. Gentrification is low-cost housing being torn down and being replaced with condominiums which poor people can't afford. It's upgrading. Displacing the people who lived there before, pushing them out and squeezing them right out, changing the neighbourhood and making it too expensive."

"For people on fixed income, like myself, not having to pay rent frees up my life incredibly. Working and having to pay rent, getting welfare money or UI, means spending 50 percent, sometimes two-thirds, on rent. It isn't right. You have to put all that energy into working, just to pay rent. By squatting, you free yourself of so much misery. There's a lot more you can do to the place that you move into to make it comfortable for yourself. Before history everyone squatted."

"I think squatting fits into anti-consumerist philosophy and into environmental issues. All these wasted buildings. One of the reasons squatting isn't seen as a positive thing by some rich people is because it doesn't fit into the consumer thing, which is part of what is keeping them rich."

"It's the developers that are really calling the shots on this one it seems. The reasons the condominiums are getting built is because of the logic of the marketplace—the only way right now developers can make money is by building high-priced condos. There's no money to be gained from low-rental housing. You're going to make the most money out of condos.

"Actually it goes further than the logic of the marketplace. It goes into the logic of capitalism, which sees housing—which is such a basic right or necessity—as a commodity that can be used purely for profit. These developers are playing games; it has nothing to do with people.

"But we don't feel helpless even though we're homeless. There are groups to help the poor like charities. The charities need to help somebody to make the charities feel good. But the effect they have on the people is often patronizing. The Salvation Army, they want you to sit through this religious service to save you, but actually to imprison you in this misery of poverty. I have been homeless many times, sleeping outside. Then I discovered lawn furniture."

"Some of the people here are staying until it's demolished. There's no reason it should be left empty or made uninhabitable before an actual demolition permit is issued."

As I was saying goodbye when we had finished taping, two women came by. I told them I would like to hear what the women have to say. I had only found men at that point who were ready to talk. The women didn't trust me either. We sat down on an old discarded picnic bench and had a conversation where we discussed who we knew mutually. I was accepted and these women told me about their women's only squat house.

"I'm squatting because I need a home. It's scary. There's a certain amount of vulnerability going to bed at night, wondering if the cops are going to be knocking on your door and kicking you out of your home. There's a lot of struggle and fear in deciding what you are going to say to the developer if he shows up. How you're going to work out staying for a month and a half, which isn't a long period of time, because otherwise the building might just be vacant. Trying to present it like he *should* let us stay here. It's hard to get that kind of courage. That's part of the reason why I'm staying in an all women's squat."

"It's really empowering living with these particular women. We have a policy where men are allowed in our house on Wednesdays only."

"The women in our squat are probably some of the more politically activist in this group. And our house is the messiest!
  "The squatters have got together a group called SAVE—the Squatters Alliance of Vancouver East—and we are organizing around that in the squats because there are four of these on this block. We've been working as a group and we are the only women's squat. A lot of them have mostly men. There's a lot of men and we've been dealing with the sexism, the male domi-

nance, and we've been putting our foot down, saying shape up or you'll lose our support, and if you lose our support, you're sunk."

"Like my friend said, it's really empowering to be with women. We've had this bond of communication: if one of us is feeling emotional pull from our personal lives, regardless of the vulnerability and stress we are under about the squat, we're there for each other and we are open to communication and trying to help one another regain our empowerment. I think it's been really good for all three of us. Women are conditioned to believe that we can only get our support, our provision, our information, from men. Women are very conditioned to believe that, so a lot of women, especially on the street, who see that and hear that all the time, they feel that, they live that. For us, I think we've taken an active step and we've said no, that's not true—we are strong women, and we will take control of our own lives, and we are not going to depend on men, and we *can* do it ourselves.

"Also, the three of us have talked about it a bit, because we are scared of losing one another. In between stages, when we're not sure where we are going to live, where we're having to depend on friends to put us up, we are going to keep in contact and still try to find another place, be it a squat or what."

"I don't like being homeless, but there isn't a lot of options right now. When I first came to Vancouver I was 16 and I was homeless and lived on Crab Beach. There was a lot of harrassment down there and brutality. I moved into a drug house, lived there for a few months, and then moved into the basement of a downtown bar for a few months. Not having proper affordable housing really sucks. The streets are ugly. Squatting is the most viable alternative that I see for people in my income bracket, which is zero to four hundred a month."

"With cities in general, I've had experience in different parts of Canada. You have politicians, developers, business people, and they have a tendency to not care about the poor, lower income families. A lot of times it revolves around racism as well, where the government wants to control large sections of people who are different, whether they be poor people, women, people of colour. They target a certain area that they think may be able to bring a higher price, and they ghettoize the people that live in those neighbourhoods so they're easier to control. It's a form of control, and a horrendous case of oppression. They just don't care about poor people or lower-income or people of colour or women at all."

"The city has the power to say what buildings will or won't be demolitioned—they're not using any of that power to protect the housing. They want this place to look like Chicago or Toronto or Los Angeles or New York City—just a conglomerate of high-rise brick buildings—and it's not going to have any grass, any trees, and it's really disgusting. Ask the city what they have the power to do and why they are not doing it. Ask the province, since they have the power to do it, why they won't. The province won't put any regulations on rent increases. They say that it's marketing. That just won't do for the working poor or unemployed."

Do you have a message you would like to give women who are homeless in transition houses or shelters, or who are facing problems of being evicted?
"Listen to what we are saying, hear the empowerment we have. They should check out the women in their lives and get together to regain that power, because they have that power. We have that power. We all have it. We don't need to sell ourselves. Everyone has a right to housing and we shouldn't have to raise our skirts and say, 'I'll have sex with you if you'll put a roof over my head for a night.' I think it's a sad alternative. If street women got together as a group, they could recognize their own power and they could take control."

This interview took place in the yard behind the houses. We sat on an old abandoned picnic table. The sun was shining, it was so comfortable sitting, talking with these women. It was good to hear them say *This is wrong;* women shouldn't have to give their body for a place to sleep. Affordable housing is a right. The developers have no moral right to run us, the poor, out of our communities.

I walked back up Commercial Drive. I had lived there for quite a few years. How I missed the community, the coffee shops, La Quena, the graffitti on the walls, the posters, the mixture of people. I had been living in an attic suite that I heated with a gas stove. I was constantly sick with asthma and bronchitis. The rent was much more than my shelter allowance from welfare. I had to use my food money towards the rent. When I eventually, after a long wait, got into social housing, it was clean, warm, cheap. My bronchitis cleared up and so did the asthma. It was out of my community, though, and it was very difficult to adjust. I really feel the Commercial Drive area is my home. I know it's going to change, that developers are taking over.

What does the word developer mean? To develop should mean to improve. Instead they often create treeless, cement, pastel-shaded jungles.

Press Statement from Squatters Alliance of Vancouver East

We are some of many squatters in Vancouver who are occupying several of the hundreds of habitable houses left vacant by developers. These houses have been slated for demolition and gentrification.

Gentrification means the construction of high-price condominiums or other dwellings and the destruction of affordable housing accompanied by the displacement of previous residents.

We feel that the displacement of longtime residents is totally unacceptable and that the new developments are intentionally beyond the price range of working poor and unemployed peoples in Vancouver and, in a lot of cases, beyond the means or extremely financially straining on the middle class.

In the face of unregulated rent increases, and out of necessity, we have chosen to squat as one of many viable means of protesting this atrocity.

These houses being habitable and unoccupied, in a time of an extreme housing crisis in Vancouver, is criminal. Housing is not a luxury, it is a right, and these houses are available NOW.

Habitable houses should not be left unoccupied while developers await approval of demolition permits, which sometimes takes many months. Since developers are making nothing from these unoccupied houses, it is obvious that it is not the money they are concerned about. Therefore, these houses should be available free of charge to those willing to maintain the premises and thereby preventing these houses from becoming criminal havens, shooting galleries, or drug houses.

Demolition of houses should only proceed with the guarantee that construction will begin within 30 days. This prevents the current situation of vacant lots being left undeveloped for several months where habitable housing used to stand.

New developments must be kept within an affordable price range for all peoples presently affected by the housing crisis.

People in a neighbourhood slated for re-zoning, gentrification or development should be part of the decision-making group that approves or disapproves such construction. People did not move into these areas to be neighbours with a high rise condominium but to be a part of a community.

We are currently organizing various neighbourhood-inclusive community events and activities (i.e. potluck barbecues, daycare facilities, community gardening and recycling projects) in an effort to open up communication between squatters and paying tenants and homeowners.

We intend to defend these houses and hope to keep them standing indefinitely as a way of preserving our neighbourhoods.

We have been forced to go public at this time because we are in danger of losing our homes. The owner/developer of our houses is demanding that we pay rent but will not allow us tenant status. We feel this is an outrage. We are not opposed to paying rent, but only accompanied by tenant's rights.

The Frances Street Squats
by Keith Chu

Word spread quickly about the four empty houses on Frances Street and, building by building, all of them were squatted within three weeks.

It was the end of February when I moved in and the insecurity of it all was what hit me the most at first. We were living in a limbo of not knowing what rights we had or what legal procedures were necessary to evict us. Our response bordered on paranoia. (This paranoia was fueled by stories of other squats in Vancouver

Three of the houses squatted on Frances Street in 1990

where, for instance, things had been quiet for two months and then the squatters had come home to find workers chucking all their possessions into dump trucks.) For all we knew, the landlord could show up with sheriffs or police to evict us at any time of the day or night. And so we only entered in the backway through the alley, we changed locks on doors, some of us had secret knocks for a week or two, we were ready to pack up on five minutes notice, and we all prepped ourselves for a lightning eviction. We put blankets over top the curtains to keep light from getting out at night. (It was argued back and forth about whether it would be openness or secrecy that would get us into trouble.) A cop car parked outside the houses for a few minutes (as happened two or three times) was enough to call an emergency meeting.

Still, my room—spacious with hardwood floors and broad windows which the sun rose through—and of course the rentlessness of it all made it worthwhile. All the houses were in solid condition (one of them could be called beautiful), and had a healthy number of years left in them. We got our Hydro hooked up, some of us had telephones, and of course water, stove, fridge, etc.

My house stood empty for five months before it was squatted. Two of the houses had been tenanted by families, one for eight years, the other for twelve. Their landlords didn't tell them anything about the fact that they were selling the houses and then, boom, out of nowhere, they were given two months to vacate. Now all four houses plus two others in the same row are owned by a developer, Ning Yee (who has been responsible for several developments in the area), who plans to demolish the houses for condominiums.

The fences separating the houses were the first to go. A donated washer and dryer were installed in one of the squats to serve as a communal laundromat. A free store ("Take what you need. Leave what you can") was started in one of the garages and began thriving by word of mouth. Squatting posters became commonplace up and down Commercial Drive.

To survive as squatters, working closely together is necessary. Meetings were frequent and long. When we should declare ourselves publicly was a matter of intense discussion. Plans of action were formulated. Information on the legalities of squatting helped (some of) the paranoia to subside, and gave us a sketchy idea of what to expect.

I realized early on that this was the first time I had really lived in what could be called a "community." The original communities were forced out of the necessity of mutual aid for survival. Now there's no reason to talk to each other anymore—we can go to work at our alienated job working for a boss we don't like, buy all the things we need from a supermarket or shopping mall, enjoy our freedom allotments (i.e. vacation) two weeks a year, and then retreat to our homes and maybe families and barricade ourselves in and let it all fall apart around us. When you're squatting there's so much more need to co-operate, to depend on each other for basic needs (i.e. repairs, food, etc.), to support each other morally and organize ourselves politically. And there's a solidarity that comes along with having to do that. Backyard barbecues were common, we were always visiting just to hang out, and many of us talked excitedly about creating community. (That we had to consciously talk about creating something as innately natural as human community says something about how isolating this society is.) When was the last time you knew your neighbours? And liked them? Working and living so closely together with supportive people who are affirming what you're doing, everyday life is so different from the (relative) isolation that is business-as-usual.

Being in a community doesn't of course mean that you suddenly exist in a hazy utopian state of squishy, hippy harmony. The dynamic of so many people is more complicated than we've been taught to handle. We definitely had our share of internal tensions and problems with group process, but trying to overcome them is all part of learning the skills of communal living.

Around the end of March, a month into our stay, Ning Yee discovered us, much to his discombobulation. (Finding a dozen and a half organized, ornery squatters living an illegal existence in *his* buildings was not one of the best things that could happen to him as a landlord.) His first response was a Get-out-tomorrow-or-I'm-having-the-Hydro-cut-off. Instead, we arranged to meet him, to negotiate, to at least buy ourselves some time. He ranted on about free rides and respect for private property and then, finally, listed his demands. He wanted rent paid daily, a security deposit for the Hydro, and an agreement to leave on 24 hours notice (signed by us, but not by him). We held yet another meeting among ourselves. (At this point, we were averaging one a day.) We agreed to his terms and offered him the token sum of one dollar per squatter per day (hoping that if he accepted this sum, it would constitute tenancy under the Residential Tenancy Act, and he would be legally bound to give us at least two months notice to vacate, negating the 24-hour agreement). Ning Yee literally laughed at the offer and then set Easter Monday as the deadline to get out before he brought in the cops.

And so we went public. On Easter Monday, April 16, we held a community event, a Squatters' Jamboree, in the backyards of the houses. It was all at once an open house to spread information, a show of support, and a festive celebration. About 200 people from around the neighbourhood showed up throughout the day to hang out, eat the free food, talk and listen, and dance to the live music of Ngoma.

The media onslaught started the next day. The Vancouver *Sun*, the front page of the *Globe and Mail*, CBC-TV, CBC-Radio, BCTV, CKVU—most of the coverage was relatively sensitive to the issues at hand. Part of the reason the coverage was so positive was, I think, because we were presented as the "helpless homeless," driven to desperate acts by the housing crisis. We were very much "victims," and therefore acceptable. That we squat also out of choice, that squatting is a powerful action, that we are trying to create something better and to empower, all that was ignored, and if stressed would have turned us into "radicals" (i.e. bad) rather than "helpless homeless" (i.e. acceptable). Despite all this, the media definitely changed everything. Since then we haven't heard from Ning Yee and we are moving happily into our fifth month. The next day, everybody on Commercial Drive seemed to be talking about the squats. Our position was clear and the neither-here-nor-thereness of the past was dissolved.

The moral support we received from the community was resounding. The Grandview-Woodland Area Council unanimously passed a motion supporting the Frances Street squats and the concept of utilizing empty housing in general. SAVE (Squatters Alliance of Vancouver East) began receiving mail and telephone messages from people leaving addresses of empty houses they were aware of (as well as one person who gave us a key to go along with the addresses).

The most recent developments on Frances Street: Ning Yee has said to the Vancouver *Sun* that he won't be demolishing due to high interest rates. A fifth house, a big four-storey dream house, was squatted. The sixth house has tenants who were supposed to move out at the end of May; they haven't, and so they now fall into the squat category. A very successful Squat Hop was held at the Pitt Gallery, and squat gatherings will continue in the future. Summer has seen an influx of people looking for shelter, and with the growing number the chances of them spilling over into establishing new squats for themselves increases.

One thing I've found is that while there is a lot of support for squatters, there are considerably less people willing to do it. The insecurity is too much of a risk. Because there is a housing crisis, people are afraid to let go of their places, lest they get kicked out of a squat and be left with nowhere or having to pay an even higher rent somewhere else. For this reason most of the squatters are in their early or mid-twenties, are single, and don't have dependents—they are people who can afford the semi-transience of squatting. (There are several notable exceptions to this rule.) However, once that element of transience is accepted, things get a lot easier. I feel comfortable, knowing that, because I have a supportive community around me, if we do eventually get evicted, we can move to other squats just as easily.

While the bottom line for squatting is that we just plain needed housing and couldn't bear the percentage of our income that rent sucked up, all of us, I think, could have arranged some sort of alternative shelter in an emergency, probably something as simple as crashing with friends. It should be noted that there are silent multitudes of street people who squat in minimal conditions, a sleeping bag on the floor and not much else, who have been squatting since before we knew what the word meant.

The first response of most visitors is a sympathetic, "What a shame about these houses" (partly, I think, because they came expecting burned-out husks falling apart and were surprised by the solidness of the houses), and a wistful what-is-this-world-coming-to shake of the head. Then they share their own stories of evictions or rent hikes or demolished houses replaced by condominiums. They realize that the fate of these squats is part of the greater process of gentrification and yuppification, that it's not just six houses being demolished, but a whole community being destroyed. Their sad response is an acceptance of the "inevitable." If we could teach anything by squatting, it would be to show the possibility of fighting back, of taking action for ourselves, of refusing the role of victims.

Vancouver's future is New York. Some New York squatters came to visit us a few weeks ago. In the Lower East Side of N.Y. there are over 500 squatters and the area is undergoing intense gentrification. Next to the squatted apartment building they lived in was an empty lot where street people had built a shantytown consisting of a few shacks. The anaesthesia of heroin and crack was prevalent in that neighbourhood and at night you can hear screams. Gunshots are not uncommon. Still, many families squat because of unaffordable rents. In the midst of this the squatters are building hope.

We see ourselves as utilizing resources that capitalism is leaving wasted. It is one of the irrationalities of the marketplace that houses stand empty, kept vacant by laws that protect private property, while there are people that need housing. By squatting, the whole notion of accumulated property and of paying rent to landlords is challenged. Everybody in this society is becoming faced with an either/or choice—support the rights of property or support the rights of people who need housing.

I remember reading in the newspapers about Jack Poole and the Vancouver Land Corporation, about how they were going to build several hundred units of housing for moderate income earners, about their operating capital of $25 million, funded by union pensions and the city of Vancouver. Poole was quoted as saying they were going to try extra hard so that some of the one bedroom apartments might be as low as $600. It turns out that this year they'll be building less than 50 units of housing. Meanwhile, on Frances Street, twenty-five people have provided housing for themselves, with no operating capital, no bureaucracy and no rent. Imagine if $25 million was given to people to squat the several hundred buildings and apartment units left empty for months by real estate speculators, and to do their own repairs. More housing would be "created" than Jack Poole could ever dream of. The consequences for developers and speculative real estate deals would be devastating.

At one of the Frances Street Squatters' Jamborees

Instead, in other cities, developers and city councils have responded to squatters by vandalising empty houses. Electrical wiring is ripped out, toilets are plugged with cement, windows are smashed. Many developers use arson as a shortcut to meeting all the requirements for a demolition permit; some of these houses have squatters in them. In Toronto, some developers aren't just boarding up their houses, they're ripping up the floorboards. It's amazing to what lengths some will go to keep others homeless.

In the midst of all this, squatters are creating an ethically based alternative within a society that venerates hyper-materialism while class disparities widen and ecological destruction threatens basic survival. While quite a number of us work, many of us are opting out of the 9 to 5 that rent necessitates in order to do something more creative, build something more useful.

We are inspired by squatting movements elsewhere, where squats have been the home base for alternative movements to develop. In West Germany, squatters have become a political force to be reckoned with—at its height, demonstrations to support squatters could bring 50,000 people out into the streets. In the early eighties, the Kreuzberg district of West Berlin was home to several kindergartens, an alternative school, cafés, galleries, a cinema, a pirate radio station, and music and theatre groups—all operating out of squats. Empty lots blossomed into guerrilla gardens, and a three-acre piece of land was reclaimed for a children's farm in the middle of the grey city. The scene was big enough to support a weekly squatters' magazine with a circulation of 5000 and no ads.

In Denmark, 54 acres of an abandoned naval barracks in the city of Copenhagen were squatted in 1971, and for the last 19 years have been a self-governed community of over a thousand squatters in the largest self-contained squat in the western world. In England, national squatting services give support and information to the over 50,000 squatters in that country (over 30,000 in London alone).

Squatting in Vancouver is in an embryonic stage. Right now, although housing is tight for many, there is still some room to move, but it will get tighter until finally it will be too constricting to ignore. In being forced into militancy, in utilizing the houses capitalism leaves empty, in realizing there is little government can do for us, in realizing that, in any case, we'd rather do it ourselves, in realizing all this we start a process. This process sees us reasserting control over one of the basic issues of our lives, reclaiming a free space that is our own, recreating the community that has been eroded by today's culture of atomization. This process is the birth of an alternative that can provide empowerment and hope in the face of displacement and homelessness.

We do all this every day in how we live.

Copyright © 1990 by Keith Chu. Reprinted with permission of the author.

Stats

In 1980, 65,000 families in B.C. were living in poverty.

By 1984, 120,000 families and 150,000 single people lived in poverty—about 27 percent of the population of the province.

Between 1980 and 1985, the number of people receiving GAIN increased from 125,000 to 230,000....

In 1986 there were 20,000 housing starts in B.C.
- less than 200 were private, rental, non-subsidized starts
- under 2000 were rental housing starts

from "Housing and Homelessness" by David Hulchanski in A Place to Call Home

In 1987, federal and provincial governments will fund the construction and rehabilitation of 20,000 housing units for a total of 425,000 social housing units in Canada.

from "Shelter or Homes" by H. Peter Oberlander and Arthur L. Fallick

May Day

Lotus

In late April I saw Lotus down on Hastings Street. I knew she had recently been homeless, and I asked her how she was feeling, and if she felt like talking about her experiences. She agreed and we found a spot to sit down and talk.

It's so different talking to someone who is homeless or has been homeless versus someone who is giving services to the street people. Homeless people talk slowly, reliving experiences in their minds, sometimes not talking for a minute, just lost in their thoughts. Sometimes they lose the question as they get lost in their pain. Their answers are not pat, not planned, not always politically realistic. They're simple sometimes, like saying "homeless people need homes." So it was with Lotus as she remembered the three times she was homeless. She would stop, searching for words to express a painful memory, then say after a few minutes, "I'm sorry, what was the question?"

The front-line workers are swift and articulate with their words and thoughts, and most of them know the politics of homelessness and poverty. It's so different when people are talking about their personal pain and loneliness. Pain can't be rushed. I have learned to flow with the homeless people I have talked with, not asking endless details, just accepting what they want to say.

"In Feburary I was in an abusive environment. I left with my two sons—6 years and 9 months. In the middle of the night the police called the victims' assistance. They drove me to Powell Place. I stayed there one month 'cause I couldn't go back and didn't know what to do. I was going to move out of town. I didn't want the hassle.

"It was difficult in the shelter. I am a homebody. I love my home. The lack of privacy hit me in the face. It was hard on me and my kids. There were a lot of rules that made it hard for me to stay there. Babies had to be in bed by 8:30 p.m. and you had to stay with them till they went to sleep. That took hours. The three of us had one room, bunk beds, a single bed, and a crib. Some of the workers there are overworked. The cook was great.

"A woman's sharing circle would have helped. You have to get one of the other women in the shelter to babysit for you if you need to go out. They have children already; it's hard on them. They are already stressed out. But if I was homeless again I guess I would go back there. I'd have to...

"I've gone back to the person I left to try and work things out. Things are much better. He's not drinking.

"When I was about 13 I was homeless. I crashed at friends, stayed up all night in the park. It was an adventure. Then I got sexually molested so I went home after that. I was hitch-hiking to my friend's house. This guy picked me up in his truck. He forced me to touch him. I jumped out, ran to a house, banged on the door. The people called the police. When the police arrived, one of them said to me, 'What's the matter, he didn't pay you?' The other cop said, 'Lay off of her.' My parents brought me home.

"Then when I was 14 my whole family was homeless. We all ran away from home. My mom was leaving an abusive relationship. My mom, brother, sister and me, we were driving from Saskatchewan to Vancouver. And we got stuck in Calgary. There was big snow storms and we didn't have snow tires. We ended up in an emergency shelter for two weeks. It was really crowded. We shared a large room with other families. Some of our clothes got stolen. My mom, to get us out of the shelter, took the first apartment she could get. It was old and full of cockroaches. My mom showed me my bedroom. The cockroaches were crawling up the walls. I said, 'I'm not sleeping there.' I slept in the living room on a fold-up cot. We moved to various places till we got into social housing. It was a really nice little townhouse, new and clean. I was happy."

What would be a solution to homelessness?

"A lot more social housing. Treatment centres. Long-term extended care. More sharing of homes with single moms that are compatible."

May 1:
Vancouver City Hall Demonstration

I arrived early. I have learned after all these years of demos that coffee and a trip to the washroom are always necessary for me. So there I was with my Carnegie volunteer sweatshirt, jean jacket covered with buttons that were objecting to everything, trying to be discreet. I went to the cafeteria in City Hall, then went up and sat in a chair near the Information desk, just quietly waiting for the demo to happen. It was raining outside. It didn't make any sense to wait outside for the demo buses to arrive.

This nice-looking, grey-haired man in casual clothes edged his way up to me, big smile, hat on the back of his head, about six feet tall. "Hello," he said. "How are you today?" "Fine," I said. "What time is the demonstration?" he asked. "Are you here for it?" He spoke with a big smile and a laid-back imitation of a non-stressed person. My response: "You're security, aren't you? In fact you're in charge of security and you're trying to pretend you're not, right?"

He admitted to being in security, and asked me if I was in charge. I told him I had just come in to use the washroom and get coffee. He didn't believe me and he wasted a lot of time trying to prove I was in charge, directing anyone that had a question to me. One of the young squatters that I had met came in and sat beside me, and we talked about the squats.

City Hall was packed with people protesting city housing policy. It was really strange and quite unique to see the affluent from Kerrisdale, Kits, and the west end, and the east end groups united. The squatters were there too. They threw a banner over the balcony upstairs in City Hall. I'm telling you, the place was jumping.

The mayor wasn't there, so Carole Taylor mayored. She dressed, as usual, in what was appropriate for the occasion—an outfit to meet demonstrators in. She sat poised, dignified, her makeup never cracking. She observed the masses, sort of queenlike. We hissed and booed at appropriate times. The presentation was made and then we left, united in our agreement to come back.

Mayday! Mayday! S.O.S.!

This is the statement read to Vancouver city council by protesters at the May 1, 1990 demonstration.

The Housing Crisis Continues...

We are tenants and homeowners from Kerrisdale, Grandview-Woodlands, West Point Grey, the Downtown Eastside, Kitsilano, the West End, and other neighbourhoods throughout our city.

Many of us were in these Council Chambers on December 19, 1989. We told you then that we are angry at the indifference and lack of political will that has allowed the housing crisis to continue. We also told you that we believe that there are solutions to the current deeply ingrained crisis. We made it perfectly clear, over four months ago, that action is needed quickly to prevent more and more people from losing their homes. We said this action must include:

1. A temporary stop to demolitions
2. A moratorium on the closure of secondary suites
3. A rent regulation system to deal with excessive and unjustified rent increases

Our demands were clear and straightforward. We fully expected them to be heard and acted upon. We have sent out a loud and clear S.O.S. We are now giving you a *Mayday warning*. The housing crisis continues. It has become ingrained. Thousands of people have already been affected. Many more are threatened.

Up until now you have ignored us. So we are back.

We have returned because the majority of this Council continues to put bottom line profit before planning and neighbourhoods.

Consequently the demolition of affordable housing goes on. Pricey condos shoot up where affordable rentals have come down. Empty lots sprout weeds and "For Sale" signs where people's homes once stood. And across all our neighbourhoods, abandoned buildings, that previously housed hundreds of Vancouver tenants, sit boarded-up and useless.

These instant ghost towns in the middle of our communities are a constant reminder of this Council's failure to put the housing needs of Vancouver residents before the blockbusting greed of developers. Right now in the Downtown Eastside alone, approximately 1500 units of housing are threatened. Where will it end?

In East Vancouver a group of "squatters" have removed the boards from the windows and created homes. Like many others, these young people are running out of housing options. Too many people in our city are a very short step away from the street and homelessness. An empty building is a much better option than the underside of a bridge.

The squatters have found one way to deal with the affordable housing shortage. What has this Council done?

You have blindly forged ahead with the closure of secondary suites, even though these suites make up a large chunk of our rental housing stock. Neighbourhood after neighbourhood has warned you of the folly of your expensive and time-consuming suite review policy.

Yet in spite of growing resistance from both tenants and homeowners, and in the face of legal challenges, the majority of you still insist on closing decent and affordable housing in the middle of a housing crisis. In the words of a Vancouver *Sun* editorial of April 19th: "It's a mess that many voters will remember when they vote in the November civic election."

Combined with the demolitions, the suite closures create a net loss of much needed affordable housing. The result: more desperation and suffering, more discrimination, and growing "market extortion." As the population rises and the rental market shrinks, far too many landlords continue to line their pockets with exorbitant, inflated, and unjustified rent increases.

This Council persists in complaining that they do not have the power to control rents. Yet the majority of you have helped create a housing situation in which "rent gouging" has become a fact of life in our city.

We are still fed up with your excuses and expressions like: "that is not in our jurisdiction" and "we do not have the power."

The real question remains: do you have the political courage

May Day demonstration outside Vancouver City Hall, May 1, 1990

and commitment to do what is necessary to deal with a very real and very destructive housing crisis?

We do understand that a variety of measures are needed from all levels of government—federal, provincial, and municipal.

Unfortunately since our pre-Christmas visit the federal government tabled a budget which clearly showed their lack of commitment to a National Housing Policy. An already beleaguered social housing program, for example, was cut by a further 15 percent.

Meanwhile the Social Credit government continues to treat tenants as second class citizens. While expounding the virtues of a profit-driven free market, the provincial government has continued to slant the rules in favour of the land speculator, the real estate flipper, and the quick buck artist. Affordable housing is unprotected from the wrecking ball, and tenants from blatant market greed.

And what about you? What have the majority of Vancouver's City Council done to alleviate the housing crisis?

Shortly after our last visit to these chambers, Mayor Campbell (it's a shame the Mayor can not be with us today) produced a list of "38 initiatives" revealing what his administration has done to deal with what the Mayor called "a tight housing market."

Read these "initiatives." Be honest. They are at best a collection of half measures, partial truths, vague promises, and misleading statements.

The Mayor's "initiatives" read more like an election platform than a comprehensive housing policy.

In short the political rhetoric has failed to stop the demolition of affordable housing, failed to protect tenants, and failed to deliver much needed new affordable housing.

Almost a year ago Mayor Campbell trumpeted the creation of the Vancouver Land Corporation (VLC). With this scheme a large portion of city land (our land) was given over to a corporation run by a private developer, Mr. Jack Poole. Amidst the political hoopla and promises of 2000 units of affordable housing a year came criticism of the process that created the VLC, and questions of how many units, where, and at what price.

Along with Social Credit promises of new rental housing, and promises of affordable housing on the Expo and Marathon sites, the VLC remains "paper housing" to be built at some future date. And all of us in this room know that people cannot live in paper housing.

The last we heard, VLC may produce 52 units by the end of this year. How many more secondary suites will be closed by then? How many more units of affordable housing demolished?

In an April 6th letter to the editor, Mayor Campbell is now saying that it takes time to build affordable housing. If this is the case, then it is all the more important to protect the housing we already have. It makes sense.

Our existing affordable housing stock is an irreplaceable resource, one of the city's most valuable assets. Why knock housing down when it is possible to fix it up? With effective demolition controls we would not only have a necessary planning tool, but also the means to save what is valuable to the community. Then we can look at ways to replace lost units and create new housing.

You have tried to pass the buck to the federal and provincial governments. They have passed the "loony" back to you.

With the Mulroney government saying no to housing and the Social Credit saying yes to greed, it is imperative that Vancouver City Council do what is necessary to deal with the chronic crisis that has affected so many in our city. You say you do not have the power. Then demand it. If senior levels of government refuse to grant the necessary powers, then look to your own City Charter. See Section 173. You have emergency powers. Use them.

After months and months of severe crisis you still do not have a coherent and comprehensive housing plan. That is amazing. Too many of you are still looking at individual buildings in isolation, and not at neighbourhoods with real people in them. The majority of you continue to treat a major disease with bandaids.

The worst thing of all is that some of you on this Council still refuse to admit that there is a housing crisis in our city. In the *West Ender* of April 26th, for example, Alderman Price is quoted as saying that "people see one or two buildings going down and they think there is a crisis." We find this attitude appalling.

We are here today to tell you that the callousness must stop before Vancouver is turned into a bastion of wealth and privilege and not a home for people with rights.

We are here to tell you that you need an honest and effective housing policy. You need clear goals. And what we are once again saying to you today is that our demands for preserving existing housing and keeping it affordable are a way of reaching those goals. We firmly believe that our demands are constructive and positive, and would be an effective part of any housing plan.

For those of you who have forgotten they are as follows:

1. A temporary stop to demolitions until an effective program of housing protections are in place, and a sufficient supply of affordable rental, non-profit, and cooperative housing is available in the same and similar neighbourhoods.

2. A moratorium on the closure of secondary suites and the discontinuation of the present suite review program. The "suite issue" should not be dealt with in isolation, but as part of an overall neighbourhood and City housing strategy.

3. A rent regulation system to deal with excessive and unjustified rent increases. If there is a delay in establishing a province-wide system (the Socreds show no sign of doing this), the City of Vancouver should establish a municipal rent regulation process.

We have said what we need to say. It is now up to this Council to act. If you do not hear our voices we will be back in these chambers and back at the ballot box in November.

Comments from participants at the May Day Demo

"I'm here today because we are still in the middle of a housing crisis. The thing is, people always say, 'how many?' Homeless people don't want to line up and be counted. On any given evening, especially when it gets warmer, it's not only the downtown eastside where there are people sleeping out."

"I'm here today because I'm sick and tired of all the bullshit. It's about time this council took some action or the people will have to take some action. Electoral action or other kind of action."

"I think it's simply outrageous that there are people living alone with three and four bedrooms while there are children out on the street."

"Natives have a hard time finding housing. It's been like this for centuries. It's not just natives, it's poor whites too. We are supposed to be recognised by human rights as equal and should get proper accommodation."

"I believe there are not only homeless people in Vancouver, but shelterless. It's about time we were occupying public buildings for the homeless."

"I see people sleeping under the bridges and all over the place. Families too."

"Do I believe there are homeless people in Vancouver? I most certainly do. Homeless people, people who can't even find shelter at night. I'm 75 years old. I come out to demonstrate because I believe, but for the grace of God, there go I."

I asked the reporter from the Vancouver *Sun* if she believed there were homeless people?
   "Any work that I've done, I've found there are not that many homeless."

* * *

Do you believe there are homeless in Vancouver?

"Yes, I'm one of them."

Well, I've just had the reporter from the Sun *say there aren't that many homeless in Vancouver...*

"That's a bunch of bullshit. We need our own newspaper."

"I think it was discouraging to hear people lobbying to governments that don't give a shit. The government is creating class war by not taking the housing shortage seriously. We are the ones that are going to take control of our housing crisis. Squatting is the only thing I can afford. The squatters came to support, but we were not given a voice or a chance to express our opinion. Then they closed it off and said we're all going home. We didn't have a voice."

Carnegie Centre—Living Room for the Homeless

As you go into Carnegie Centre there's a round reception desk with non-uniformed security persons, men and women, who answer the phone, answer a million and one questions, take messages. At the same time they keep an eye on the door to make sure no one drunk or abusive comes in.

Hundreds of people daily pass through those doors. With free programs and cheap food, it's the living room for the people who live in small hotel rooms. Lonely people, homeless people, all kinds of people use the centre because it meets their needs. Hundreds of people go there, day and evening, seven days a week. They socialize, talk to each other, play chess or cards, dance. There are education programs, a cheap cafeteria. It's like one huge family. I have been told that you only have to be in town a month, and after three days at Carnegie you start to feel a sense of home.

I asked the woman sitting behind the counter what happens when a homeless person comes into Carnegie. She replied, "You know, homeless people that come in here often won't admit to being homeless." Sometimes someone will recognize them and try to get them helped. When people ask for help, the staff try to refer them to Emergency Services.

I know that staff have taken homeless people home. One female staff member gave shelter to a couple that were homeless. Carnegie patrons themselves help out people who are in a jam. One man told me he's on a circle and that's why he was evicted. When he was in trouble, people took him into their room, then later when they were in trouble, he took them in. Now he's evicted again. He said, "It's a never-ending circle. If they help you, you gotta help them, then they gotta help you, so we all finish out on the street." He was a man who had been in and out of detox.

Volunteers in Carnegie get coffee tickets. These tickets can buy a fruit, a sandwich, or soup. Many volunteers share their coffee tickets with the homeless and hungry.

Sometimes people are on the streets for a couple of weeks. The scenario is: welfare cheque is cashed and you pay the person you are staying with the rental portion; give welfare the receipt. Then you spend your support money (food, etc.). You may get into an argument with your landlord. If it's a hotel you're staying at, you may be evicted, so you are on the street. You can't get another welfare cheque for rent until the next month. So you survive by staying with friends or in the park, or wherever. This is a problem alcoholics and dysfunctional people face frequently. Sometimes it's an illegal eviction. Sick people who are forced to live in hotels over bars don't function well, so of course they are going to act out, of course they are going to be on the street, losing their possessions again and again.

One woman, her name is Anne, was always living in different hotels, getting evicted, going in and out of her sickness. She was often living on the street, frequently beaten and abused. For the past three years, however, she has been in safe, affordable housing. Her sickness hasn't returned and she hasn't been evicted. I saw her a few months ago and she said, "It's been so great having a nice apartment, my own kitchen. I really enjoy being home. When I lived in hotels I used to go nuts looking out on the garbage in the alleys. Do you know, now I have a view of the mountains." I was so happy to see that she was well, and that she was safe. We really need safe affordable housing to be well. If you haven't got a place to call your own, how can you be expected by society to be mentally, physically well?

Homelessness

by Paul Taylor, editor of the Carnegie newsletter

There are as many experiences and ways of coping with not having a roof over your head as there are people in the situation. The causes are usually similar, though: not enough money to pay high rents, no friend who can spare the room for a while, and all the social housing places have waiting lists a mile long.

Getting lucky, if there is such a thing as luck, almost always means being in the right place at the right time—like reading a story with a happy ending. But these stories are rare exceptions; the rule for thousands is stark reality—no room at the Inn.

The desperation can lead to excuses for extraordinary behaviour—actions that are blatantly criminal to psychotic. This sounds like a plot for a movie. It's like back in 1929 with the stock market crash: the formerly rich killed themselves; the poor just starved.

In the present day, the well-to-do bump the people who are a little less well-to-do who bump... and so on until the poorest are evicted or forced out with rents just too high for them to have a bed and eat.

At this point, the people who can do something react with an all-too-human trait—out of sight, out of mind. All across the country, especially in large cities where all the essential services are, homelessness becomes equated with poverty, something that is recognised on the surface as an embarrassment to the vaunted "system." Petty bureaucrats and hold-your-nose do-gooders become the media's favourite (or at least readily accessible) mouthpieces for getting the latest word on "What Is Being Done." Their answer: "We have identified this as a definite Problem..." Assurances are gushed that unspecified repairs are to be made in the near future by unnamed saints who have a palatable Solution to the Problem.

Time flies when you're having fun. When you're without a roof, when your security of tenure is, or could be, up within any given hour, time moves like every minute is dragged into this universe, arriving with the greatest reluctance. Only when you have to "Be Out" that day/week/month does time become an unruly monster, picking you up and throwing you to the end of the limit set at impossible speeds.

Melodramatic? Sure, when you see it on TV or it happens to someone else; when you can't even comprehend the reality of a family of four in a single hotel room, or sleeping in an abandoned car, or putting up a tent or a cardboard lean-to in a city park. This is already happening in some American cities, and Toronto and Vancouver are next. And then the rich, the bosses, the well-to-do, will call up *their* (ownership is definitely implied here) political hacks and give new orders: "Get those goddam squatters/misfits/bums...OFF MY LAND, OUT OF MY SIGHT, OUT OF MY CITY!"

Isn't it funny what animals we really are when it comes to territory.

It's hard not to generalise when it comes to pointing fingers. There are hundreds and thousands of intelligent people in positions up and down society's hierarchy who will do whatever they can to treat people as they themselves would demand to be treated. What seems to hit from the blind side is that a very small number of people will consciously and cold-heartedly stop any such social actions.

Wealth and power are two sides of the same coin...and having one means, invariably, wanting the other. Hence, we get the most prevalent mental disease of the human race—turning money into power and power into money and money into power, ad nauseam. And the poorer people struggle and flounder and get squashed under the weight of their burden—trying to live as if life had meaning and purpose.

Homelessness is the subject of this diatribe (good word if it fits), but going over what's been put down so far, we haven't left it for so much as a comma. Homelessness, poverty...these don't just happen with nothing behind them causing more and more people to feel their grip. It's not jargon or rhetoric to use phrases like "the Corporate Agenda" or "the rich get richer, the poor get poorer." It's a symptom of a human failing called greed. What will happen next is not anybody's guess; what comes next is obvious. As more intelligent and strong people are forced into poverty by rapacious weaklings, there will be a grassroots revolution which will not be cowed. It will show itself in small victories leading to networks of people leading to having issues resolved with the interests of humanity as a whole satisfied.

In another place on this planet, it's just understood as a fact of life that if a child starves or dies from want, it's the fault and responsibility of the entire society for not foreseeing the difficulty and changing everything necessary to give that child a life worth living.

Homelessness must be as temporary as it's humanly possible to make it...always.

The Men

I was concerned about a young man who stood all day near the drugstore, looking up to the sky. Dressed in rags, he just stood there every day. The drugstore and the restaurant were angry because he used their wall in the back as a urinal. It was getting really cold. He didn't wear a heavy coat. People would come and give him food, clothing, even money. He would just toss it on the roof of the one-storey restaurant.

I got to know him, talked with him. He was very gentle like a timid wild bird. He was about 26, had dark hair and deep blue eyes, and was so thin. He told me he slept in the park close by at night. I was scared he would die of hypothermia. He just had lost all touch with reality. He spoke about a worker that he had had a good relationship with. I called her, talked to the community health team, talked to as many people as I could to get help for him. He didn't want help and couldn't be forced to take help. I wanted him to get well and then decide if he wanted to freeze to death.

One day I went to look for him and he wasn't there. I was scared. I thought he must have died. I made some calls and was told he was in a shelter and was getting some kind of treatment. It's so hard to let someone go on like that when they are too sick to know what reality is.

Pierre

Pierre is on the bus, at the back, sitting in a double seat. About 35 years of age, he looks like he hasn't washed in years. He talks and smiles to himself, obviously sleeps out somewhere—I don't know where. He has his possessions in a couple of shopping bags.

I've seen him before. He likes to bug people. He takes off his hat, scratches his head, shakes it, then pretends to squash head lice on the seat (I hope he's pretending!). The first time I saw him do it, I freaked out and he knew, because he looked at me with a smile. I felt itchy all over. So when he does it today to a man that sits down beside him, I know he really enjoys the reaction he gets.

There used to be men that were glue sniffers who slept out in the bush at the back of Strathcona Gardens. They dragged in old mattresses and garbage bags, and just lived there. When anyone came near them, they moved away swiftly like frightened deer. The glue really fries their brains. It seems that, to survive, you need something to kill the pain, and glue is cheap, like Lysol, hair spray, chinese cooking wine, rubbing alcohol... a way out from the pain.

Mike

"Homelessness: a feeling that I don't really belong anywhere, that there is nowhere where I am accepted for who I am, where I don't need to constantly justify my existence to others and to myself."

James

James had been renting a houseboat with his dog. He was given a 24-hour eviction notice when the owners declared a "no dog in the area" rule, so rather than give up his dog, he became homeless. He couldn't find accommodation that accepted dogs and had a cheap rent. He had had his dog (a mid-size shepherd husky) for years. He said his dog, a really gentle friendly dog, was known in almost every bar in North Vancouver. No way was he going to part with it. James had broken his arm. His normal employment was brick work, so he wasn't working. A friend let him stay in an empty apartment building in the west end. The building had been home to 60 or more people—mostly older renters—who had room and board for $535 a month. It had been sold in 1989 to be torn down for condos to be built in July 1990. It had been empty for a year.

Al

What do you think can be done about homeless people?
"Well the first thing is to find some places to get everyone off the street. Drop the rents down, they could possibly do that too. I got a place now over at Lucky Lodge for $220. Fridge and sink and kitchen down the hallway. I only have $183 left over."
How long were you homeless?
"Six to eight months"
What did it feel like?
"Awful. It's hard. It's hard living. Hard to keep yourself in food."
How did you survive?
"Carnegie. Working hard, long hours. I worked over at Lucky Lodge for a little while. Get ten or fifteen dollars over there."
Where do you sleep when there's nowhere to go?
"Could be under the bridge. Could be in the parks, down by

the train station. Could be anywheres. The worst place was under the bridge."

How many years have you been homeless, on and off?
"About ten years."
Were you ever hurt?
"I was assaulted. I was hurt. I don't trust anyone. I get beat up almost every day. Coupla bruises, black eyes, one broken arm, maybe two, but not that serious. Didn't put me in the hospital anyway."
What's the solution to homelessness?
"People don't got that much money if they keep raising the rent up. I know one place that's already doing it ten dollars this month, another five dollars next month. If they keep doing that there be hardly nobody living nowheres..."

Danny

"When I was about fourteen I lived on the streets in Winnipeg. I survived by doing little errands for people like cleaning up yards and things like that. My parents worried about me. They didn't want me living on the street. I just carried on that way for quite some time. I slept between garbage cans. Sometimes I'd roll over a garbage can, crawl inside of it. I'd lay inside of it. That was my shelter, finding plastic and things like that.

"I was scared. Scared of people all of the time. I really didn't know what I wanted, because of my education too. I was quite confused at the age of sixteen. You don't know what to do. I heard the climate was much nicer out here. How did I do out here? Welfare helped me out. That was one way of being sheltered I guess.

"I'm doing okay, now. I've started to worry about myself. I try really hard to get what I want out of life. I'm not so confused anymore. I'm getting older. My health is important now. But I do feel sorry for people that are out there, living on the street. There's one lady down the street, I always see her on Granville, she has a shopping cart, she's got it all piled full of garbage. I asked her one time, what's in that carriage? She said, this is my home, this is my bed in here, this is my little belonging that I find in the garbage. I asked her, how do you find food? She told me she goes to the 7-11 and asks them if they have any food that they are throwing out in the garbage. It's one way she survives, by going to the 24-hour stores.

"I always walk down Pender—it seems more quieter down there—and I do see occasionally, in an alley—like, reminiscing, I always look up alleys to see if there are any kids down there and, yeah, once in a while you will find a kid either down an alley or something like that. Like me. I guess these are my haunts."

Peter

"Beans," he said, "that's what would be good, beans...beans ...available all day long so there wouldn't be a line-up."

I was talking to two men who had been homeless. One man, a friend, said. "Peter over there, he's been homeless for months." I looked over at the medium height, thin man, sitting quietly at another table. I said to my friend, "I'd really like to talk to him. Would you introduce me?" So he called Peter over.

I asked Peter if he had any solutions for homeless people. That's when he responded "beans." I asked him if I could tape him. He said no, firmly, he didn't want to be recorded. I was scared that he would leave. Most homeless people don't seek publicity. So I gently asked if I could write, explaining who I was and what I was trying to do. The other men assured him that I was okay, so he agreed. He was a thinking man. He took his time before speaking. He was in no hurry with his thoughts.

"I don't want welfare, there's too many strings. I sleep out in parking lots and under bridges. I've been homeless now for ten months. I don't want welfare, too many strings. Should be shelters that ask no questions... with a flop house in the back for the drunks. Could be some fights though. There used to be flop houses.

"Food is the problem, it's so hard to find good food. Lots of cakes with sugar on them. Too many cakes, not enough beans or meat. It's hard finding good food." (I know what he means. Stale baked goods are donated in the community and get doled out to hungry people. For a couple of weeks a while back we were innundated with donated Nanaimo bars. Everywhere I went in the downtown eastside, there they were.)

Peter said, "Sometimes Jim gets submarines from a dumpster, but Jim's having a hard time because they are locking the dumpsters." Twenty-four-hour stores and fast food restaurants put a lot of unsold food in dumpsters. Peter said Jim would salvage some of the food and bring it to share with them. They were waiting for him to show up. Maybe he'd have some subs.

The other man at the table said, "Peter's a great mechanic. He gets things from the dumpsters and fixes them. He can fix anything."

Peter said, "Yes, I like getting things and fixing them. There's a few of us that do the dumpsters."

I was starting to get the idea that there was a collective happening. Someone was finding food, someone was finding stuff and fixing it, trying to survive outside the system—this system that has so much to throw away, and if you can't pay for it, they'd rather let it rot on a garbage dump than let some hungry person have it for free. I guess that's what you call the marketplace. Locked dumpsters. We throw so much food away.

I asked Peter if I could talk to him again at another time. He replied, "I don't think so."

Interviewing homeless people who choose to be invisible isn't something I can arrange. I just have to be there and hang around, run into them. And then someone will say to me, "That person is homeless." Peter was clean, articulate, polite. If the other men hadn't told me, I would never have known he was homeless. Being homeless doesn't always show. Many homeless people just blend in with the community and you would never know unless they chose to let you know. Anyway, Jim never showed up with the subs, so I don't know if he got into the locked dumpsters. I asked these men what were their thoughts on the homeless women out there. They replied, "It's really hard on the women. It's not so bad for us, but women get beat up a lot. It's not very good."

Dave

Dave heard I was doing something about the homeless. Someone had given my number to him because he was about to become homeless again. A middle-aged man with a university background, he said he was classified as mentally handicapped by welfare. "I'm a scavenger," he said. "I can live off of dumpsters. I take bags of good clothes to the S.A. that I find in the garbage."

He picks up food that the supermarkets toss out. He claimed he could find $300 of groceries in one night. "They try to lock it away from the scavengers, but we get it." He has been homeless many many times. He knows how to survive on the street. He was evicted from his home before, and two tons of his salvaged "stuff" was bulldozed. He said he still had another two tons that he had managed to keep. Now he was being evicted again. If he couldn't get a home, he had plans to find somewhere and squat. He enjoyed being a scavenger. He often feeds other poor and homeless people from the food he gets from the dumpsters. He just can't stand to see all the usable stuff that people throw into the garbage. I think scavenger is an old word and the new word is recycle. People who saved good stuff from the garbage were labelled as crazy and deviant, and now we know they were right and it's quite acceptable to be a recycler.

Frederick

"I was quite surprised when I got the notice from the manager stating that they were closing [Silver Lodge] down because the city didn't issue them a permit. I heard stories that they wanted to close the place down to set up a first-class hotel, so I wasn't totally surprised. The letter looked quite suspicious to me, but I checked into it with the DERA offices, and they said the city wasn't aware about their permit. They checked it further and said that what was happening was, the fire department had taken them to court for little things like leaving a dresser out in the hallway while they were painting a room, and garbage being left on the fire escape while someone was cleaning out the garbages.

"What I think is happening is the City is just coming down on them, they want to close the place. I don't know where I'll go. There's quite possibly 75 people [in Silver Lodge], and just recently the Ohio Rooms burned down, and there are 35 left homeless because of that fire.

"I see it everyday. I see people sleeping on the streets when I'm coming home at night. I've heard stories about people being homeless for all kinds of different reasons—money, family problems, you name it. There is a problem.

"I was homeless once for about a month, but I stayed with some friends in their bus—they had a bus on their property. I hadn't seen them for a few years, and they didn't actually realize what my situation was. They thought I was just out there to visit them and to reacquaint myself with them. It was devastating. When they did realize what my situation was, I was embarrassed and ashamed. I couldn't face them after they found out, so I left.

"I'm optimistic I'll find something, but not the same kind of accommodation for what I'm paying. I've got two large rooms here at $270."

Joe

I was talking to some homeless men I have gotten to know. They said, "See that guy over there? You should talk to him. He's homeless, but when he opens his mouth you can't shut him up." They introduced me to Joe. He had long red-blonde hair and was about 48 years old. He'd been living out for about 20 years off and on. He said he just couldn't handle hotel rooms. They were so small. He had been in every city in the states, across Canada to Nova Scotia, but he had chosen Vancouver. He had a '65 car. He got a hotel room so that he could park his car and sleep in it, and use the room to store his stuff. He said his room turned into a flop house and he was evicted and he lost all his stuff and his car was impounded.

This man managed in ten minutes of conversation to trash every racial minority that I know. He was the most racist person I have ever encountered. He was a hobo Archie Bunker. I tried to be non-judgmental, but I lost out and would have loved to have told him where to go. I didn't because obviously his head was screwed up. He scratched the whole time I was interviewing him, so I didn't get too close. Book or not, I do have my limit.

Charles

Charles has been "dry" for nine years. He spent a lot of time on the street. He's in his late thirties, and is someone I've known for a few years. He's always ready to help people.

"My definition of homelessness? Well, there's people who have to do it out of necessity. They have no other choice... Then there's the people who do it because they choose to live that way.

There's an old saying that says home is where the heart is, and as long as you have someone to confide in, friends and that, you can make most any place home.

"I was about 16 or 17 when I first lived on the street. At that time, my dad was an alcoholic. We got along great, except minor problems like he wanted me in by 9; I wanted to be in by midnight or 9 the next morning, one or the other. I was working, figured I'd get my own place, couldn't pay the rent, couldn't live on my own. Everything went downhill so I was out on the street. That's about the way it went... it seemed like a lot of fun at the time, but a few years down the road, when I found myself stealing, getting in trouble, my apartment turned into a flop house—a few years down the line it wasn't funny anymore, it wasn't a lot of laughs, but then I didn't give a damn. I was so strung out on drugs it didn't matter what happened.

"What I've been through...I had friends at my side, but I wouldn't want to do it all by myself. I was a drug addict. I almost died a few times from overdoses. If it wasn't for friends picking me up and taking me to hospital and stuff...they could have just left me on the street. They took me to hospitals or to shelters and stuff...Personally they [hospitals and shelters] all suck because no one knows what they're talking about. They've never been through it. They have all these guidance counsellors and they've never been drug addicts, on the street, so how the hell do they know what you're talking about?

"They're spending billions and billions of dollars, all this space shuttle stuff and everything, all this nuclear armament and all that crap. The only thing I can say is they should spend a little more in their own backyard, open up 24-hour-a-day help centres, have it like an emergency thing, have a doctor on at all times for someone who did an overdose. Then give that guy, when they straighten him out or whatever, give him an option. Put him in the same building, as a matter of fact, have beds upstairs, drying out, detox. Give him treatment and that, and don't turn your back on him because he's been there once or twice. Sometimes it takes a few times.

"It took me about seven times. I just woke up one morning, just about to put a needle in my arm, saw myself in the mirror. I weigh 178 now. I was down to 122 pounds, looked like a skeleton with skin. So finally I just said fuck it. That was it; I threw it away, in the toilet. Put the needle in the garbage and walked away from it... and I've never done it since. Nine years, but I don't think I would have made it without the beer. I traded one crutch in for another.

"When you're on the street, you don't have a hell of a lot of friends. A couple that you think you can trust. The minute your back's turned, they'd probably stab you in the back anyway. I didn't lose my friends. In fact, I had a few come to me for help after that, asked me questions about what to do, where to go and stuff. And I helped them and that. I was kind of lucky I never got pinched for drugs, but I did go to jail a few times... once I even volunteered to go to jail. I was so strung out and that. So I hit a cop right in the mouth. I got thirty days for that. I was so strung out and I wanted to clean up my act. But as soon as I got out of jail and hit the streets and everything, then I was right back into it. I had good intentions, but they fell through. I slept in bushes and stuff, on park benches, doorways, underground parking lots, almost anywhere."

I don't understand, if people are sleeping out on the street, how they have money for drugs? They can't afford a room, they can't afford food...

"They can panhandle, they can steal, they can run around picking up bottles... That was before. Now people are robbing places, mugging and everything, for money—because it's so damned expensive. When I was doing it, it was only 20 bucks for a cap of heroin. I could get stoned twice on it. Now it's something like 60 or 80 bucks a hit. They'll do almost anything to get their money.

"I was going to compare it [cocaine] to heroin, and that's because I was a heroin addict. I've tried coke and everything when it first came out. They didn't have crack when I was around, and we were freebasing and that, but now from some of the friends that I've seen stoned—like, I still have friends who are drug addicts—and when I see them stoned, I can imagine what they're going through. Personally, I think it's three times worse. You get addicted a lot faster to crack. It's a different stone. You seem to enjoy it more. Like, heroin, you do one hit—it could be a couple of weeks before you do another one, then another one and another one and finally you get hooked, and you're doing it two or three times a day. But with crack and that, you smoke it once or twice and, bang! Or you do a needle, you don't want to let it go... Cocaine's the only drug in the world where you can have two pounds sitting in front of you and you won't stop until it's gone.

"I don't know how smart it is, or words of wisdom, but this comes right from the heart. There are places out there where you can get help. I don't think there's enough, but there are some. If you really really want to get off of it, go to a street priest, a street worker... go to one of these help groups, addiction centres. You'll think that most of them don't know what the hell they're talking about, but give them a shot. If you really want to quit, they can help you.

Pierre

I saw Pierre, the homeless man that likes to squish his lice (real or otherwise) on bus seats. He was sitting in the bank doorway, sheltering from the rain. He was wet. I said, "Hi. It's cold." He agreed. I asked him if he'd slept out the night before, if he had a home. His response: "You want to take I home with you?" I realized that English wasn't his first language and that he had misunderstood and thought I was trying to pick him up. I replied, "No, but have a good day." Didn't get that interview...

May

The man who does all of the recycling phoned me. He's the one that had fed so many hungry people with food salvaged from food store dumpsters. He was desperate, talking fast, almost crying...He was being evicted. He said, "All the stuff I've been recycling, they're putting it back in the garbage. They're here. I've tried to stash some stuff with my friends. I wanted to keep in touch with you to let you know what's happening to me." I asked him to meet me at Carnegie. He didn't show. I guess he was too busy trying to find a solution, a place for his enormous amount of salvaged items. I asked him where he was going to live; he said he didn't know.

At Carnegie Library you don't need ID or a regular library card to take out a book. I was chatting with one of the librarians and he told me that, when they were looking through their card file, the librarians noticed one man had listed his address as "under the Georgia Viaduct." They figured that whoever filed it hadn't noticed the significance of that address.

I went to talk to Dorothy at the Evelyne Saller Centre, the old 44, on Alexander. It was packed with people eating a good solid breakfast for $1.50—oatmeal, sausage, eggs, bacon, toast, juice, and coffee. The 44 offers facilities for showers, laundry, delousing, a TV lounge. There's lunch for a buck and a half, supper for $2.50. They're open seven days a week, early morning to late at night. The staff does a lot of referral work and administers monies for people who can't do it themselves, and provides other services.

There were at least seventy people there, eating. Many of them looked as if they had slept out all night. As I talked to Dorothy, we were sitting at a table with other eaters. The man across from me said, "I slept outside. I couldn't handle the stresses of the hotel, the noise, people hassling you, banging on your door."

Dorothy told me that during last winter's cold spell, the centre stayed open all night. It was packed with homeless people who had no place to stay, who came in to keep warm and just stayed up all night. She was concerned about the number of people who had obvious mental sickness, that were not taking their medication or being supervised. She said there were more and more of these people. The numbers were growing and some of them were violent. She told me she had just got a phone call from a man in Kitsilano who had a business that was going under and who couldn't afford his rent. He asked her, "Where will I go? Where will I live? I have to move into the downtown eastside, but I don't know where to go. Can you help me?"

She told me a man came to see her. He was hungry, had no place to go, was on crutches. He was black and blue and had just spent three weeks in the hospital. He was on unemployment insurance, had had a few drinks, leaned out of his window for some reason or other, and fell four stories. When he came out of hospital, all his stuff had been junked or stolen. He had been evicted. Dorothy arranged for him to eat his food at the centre, and got help to find him a room until his cheque came. He came back to see her recently. He is sober, has a good job. He told her, "If it wasn't for you, and the care I got from this place, I'd be dead."

I talked to a young man I know. He's about twenty. I asked him if he had ever been homeless. He said, "Yes, yes, many times, but I just can't talk about it. I just get depressed." I asked him what his definition of home was. He said, "A place to put your feet down, that's your own."

At Carnegie I talked to two single mothers who had been homeless. They both said that so many women are staying in abusive relationships because even if you go into a shelter, the chances of renting something agreeable at welfare rates are slim.

A homeless man outside the Army & Navy store on Hastings had a contraption of two bikes and a shopping cart. He was bearded and had long black fingernails. I said, "Hi, it's cold to sleep out." He replied, "I could get a room at a dorm but the night watchman wakes me up every couple of hours." He told me he'd been in places where the cockroaches were so thick they looked like a carpet. I asked him what he thought about homelessness. He replied, "Three years and we still do 100 percent." I asked him what he meant and he told me to think about it. I did, but I still can't figure out what he meant.

It's now the middle of May and I'm hearing rumours that real estate is cracking somewhat, though that won't help the people I've been interviewing very much. I have fantasies of condominiums being offered to welfare recipients for welfare rental rates, and the Hotel Vancouver taking in difficult-to-house people. The reality is we won't ever get back all that rental stock that was bulldozed. The governments have allowed all this to happen. Greed has taken over—but maybe the greedy are going to lose out. I'll wait and see.

The book is taking shape now; it's not a study, it's not a research paper, it's really just an intimate inside look at homeless people and people who try to bring about some changes—front-

The early morning soup kitchen at First United Church

line workers and their non-traditional social work. I am hoping it will be a voice for the homeless and the people committed to change.

When I first started to think about writing a book on homelessness, I thought I could take on the world...Canada...B.C., but I realize now that I only have to look closely at what is happening right under my nose. I'm sure what happens here happens in most cities.

I went for a walk near Main and 25th early one morning, and saw Pierre. He was lying down in the parking lot, shivering, wearing the same clothes he always wears. When I came back on my way home, he was gone. He looked in really rough shape.

West End Saturday night: four men push shopping carts full of their possessions, happily drunk, singing and laughing as they go to bed down in Stanley Park for the night. There are so many men around the West End these days with shopping carts; not with groceries but with their life's possessions. This was the first time I had seen four together. They went rolling down the sidewalk. Everyone moved swiftly out of the way. They weren't bothering anyone, just having a good time—like the guys in their BMWs, playing their loud radios, driving down Robson. Saturday night party time.

I went by the houses on Frances Street. The squatters are still there.

Tenants are really becoming militant. This week tenants on Commercial Drive went on a rent strike when their landlord wanted to raise rents from $350 to $500 a month. The apartments were in substandard condition, with tenants doing their own repairs. One woman spent $2300 on repairs. She said there had been wires hanging out of the walls and ceilings. Tenants said the place was a fire trap. The tenants were prepared to accept a 10 percent rent increase; a 43 percent increase would make many of them homeless.

Mike Harcourt, the provincial New Democratic Party leader, said there are thousands of people suffering high rent increases. The NDP has pushed for the return of rent controls and the return of the rentalsperson. It's strange how, when we make some noise, when we fight against injustice, when we say we ain't gonna take it, unhearing ears of politicians open. Mayor Campbell is having meetings with federal minister Alan Redway regarding Vancouver's housing shortage. Why doesn't he clean up his own act, too, and simply stop demolitions, stop making people homeless. Why doesn't he take control from the marketplace that is making us homeless?

The city has ordered three more hotels closed—52 units of inexpensive rooms—for failing to meet the standards. Acting mayor Carole Taylor says the 44 tenants can probably relocate to comparably priced units in the same area. Alderwoman Libby Davies wants the city to buy some of the remaining rooming houses. Two of the hotels were bought 18 months ago, and the new owners want to sell rather than do repairs. There is so much evidence of land speculation, and nobody makes any provision for the low income tenants—as I am saying too often. I have no choice but to keep on repeating it. It's the voice of the poor.

One third of the front page of the May 24 *Province* is taken up with the headline "No Let Up for B.C. Renters—Lowest Vacancy Rate in the Country." There is a 1 percent vacancy rate. We have won first place and Ontario is second with 1.3 percent.

Outside Vancouver it's equally horrendous, with .7 percent in Victoria (Toronto is .7 percent too). Mission is zero vacancy. Vernon, Kelowna, Chilliwack, and Comox have .1 percent.

Mayor Campbell is quoted as saying his council's housing policies are "easing the crunch." If this is so, why hasn't he stopped the demolitions? Why is he closing "illegal" suites?

Montreal, Toronto, the U.S., and the World

I was elected to represent End Legislated Poverty at a conference of the Pro-Canada Network in Quebec. There would be representatives from churches, labour, anti-poverty groups, aboriginal groups, and others. I thought it would be a good place to find out about the corporate agenda as it concerns homelessness. It would also be a great opportunity to stop off in Montreal and network with people involved in the homeless shelters for women that I had been part of developing fourteen years before.

Montreal in the 1970s

It was the Year of the Woman. I was working in a social work agency as a community worker. My area was the downtown core. I was aware that there were many services for homeless men—soup lines, drop-ins, etc.—but almost nothing for women. I visited these missions and asked the people who ran them: "Where do women go?" I was told over and over again that there weren't very many homeless women. One mission did allow one table to be set aside from the men so that women could eat at it.

I went to some of the established women's volunteer groups; they too, at the time, didn't agree there was a need to shelter homeless women. Women that were homeless often, as now, had no choice but to use their body for a bed, sometimes having to service as many as five men. Beatings, gang rapes, murders, and freezing to death in Quebec winters were their lot.

Doris was an alcoholic woman that I used to see around the community of Atwater, St. Antoine and Rockheads Paradise Bar. She was always giving the police obscene gestures. The headlines in the paper showed a woman had been murdered. It was Doris. She had been raped by more than one man, and brutally murdered, in a shed on St. Urbain Street. Her murderers were never found.

I went to visit a woman in jail. She had been nicknamed Grace Kelly. She had been arrested so many times for vagrancy and other minor charges that when it reached 100 times, she became a court celebrity. An elderly, grey-haired woman, clean and sober in jail, she could have been anyone's mother.

I felt I had to do something, so I organised a committee of really talented people who could do the things we needed to open a day shelter. Phil Davies was a great writer of proposals, Aileen Ross was a retired sociologist. I found a volunteer accountant from a credible firm, and some other people that could contribute more than just sitting on their asses on a committee going nowhere. We were given a government LIP grant. We found a small location next to the bar where the local sex and drug trade happened. It was the community, near the men's mission, where I had talked to the women.

We hired staff. The rent and wages were due, and as it is with governments, there was a delay, so I had to take out a personal bank loan to cover the costs. I was a single mother, so that was a difficult decision. But I had no choice; if I believed there was a need, then I had to have faith in what I was doing. So when the government money came in the next month, the loan was paid back instantly, and for years after I had one hell of a good credit rating.

Of course there were homeless women. They had a place to go now, and they were no longer invisible. So many horror stories, so much abuse, so much loneliness... it would take a whole book just to tell it all. One elderly woman had been a maid in Westmount for thirty years. When the family didn't need her anymore, they turned her out. She was too old to get more work, she became disoriented, lost, had spent some time sleeping under a bridge in a park near where she had been employed. Her homelessness had made her mentally sick. Often it's the poverty and the homelessness that drive a person crazy, not the other way around.

Chez Doris was a day shelter. The committee produced a proposal for a 24-hour women's shelter. We tried and tried, but no one would fund it.

The Grey Nuns had a convent, a square city block bounded by Mathew Street, Guy Street, Dorchester Street, almost to St. Catherine Street. Marguerite D'Youville, founder of the Grey Nuns, was a woman whose husband was a drinker. He left her owing a lot of money. She was a single mother born in 1701, so obviously she didn't have many choices. She was, I believe, one of Canada's first woman organizers. She organized shelters for the sick and homeless, and even organized a hospital. She started the Grey Nuns, and in 1990 was sainted.

One afternoon I met Soeur Georgette Leduc at a meeting that was held at the Grey Nuns' convent. While I was there I kept thinking, all this fucking space, and women are out there on the street. I told her how I felt, told her about the need and asked her what were they doing with big iron bars, keeping the homeless out, when the original Grey Nuns worked with the homeless and poor?

She took the proposals and soon the Grey Nuns agreed to start a night shelter: Maison Marguerite. I knew there would be problems of religion, but this was a coalition, and the joining thread was homeless women and their need for a place to sleep. So I, scarcely even a Protestant, English-speaking, joined up with a French Catholic nun. She was different. She too had to struggle with the fears of other nuns who were scared they would all be murdered in their beds if they let homeless women in. It wasn't easy.

In the afternoons I would be working with street people. I got to know some of the hookers on the corner, and would do referrals in the bar. In the morning I would go over to the Grey Nuns. They were two different worlds, and I had to watch my tongue with the four-letter words.

My youngest daughter was very sick. The doctors couldn't guarantee how long she would live, so the nuns prayed for her. By this time I had really got to like Marguerite D'Youville, so I put in a request for my daughter to get well, for shelters for the homeless—and my daughter did get well, and the shelters did happen. But I and others also worked very hard and put enormous energy into it.

In the basement of the convent there is a really old room. As you enter, you see row on row of grey crosses, graves. Nuns are buried there, row after row. Nuns that died from nursing sick people, many of them died young. I wasn't scared as I walked

Soeur Georgette Leduc and Sheila Baxter, in the 1970s

amongst their graves to the empty coffin of Marguerite D'Youville. It was covered in glass, and inside were little pieces of paper, yellow and brown with age, prayers and requests that had been put in over the years. Nearby, the heart of a brother or priest was preserved in a large glass jar. This is where I would talk to Marguerite. There is a small chapel upstairs, with candles and a tomb with a replica of Marguerite, which is where most people go, but for me my closest communication with Marguerite was there in that grey basement with the buried nuns.

Of course there were some things I didn't like about Maison Marguerite, given that I would have preferred a shelter with no religious ties. But this surely was better than being left on the street, and as I predicted, many women needed that shelter. There were hundreds of sick, poor, battered, homeless women. The police got to know us and would refer people to us. Social work agencies and churches sent us women. The homeless women were visible at last. It wasn't smooth, trying to relate to the attitudes of some of the staff at Maison Marguerite; we definitely had different ideas on how a shelter should run. But it was so much better than the street. The food was good, the rooms were bright and cheerful.

Now it's 1990. I went back to visit Chez Doris. It has done very well. The staff and board have struggled through some hard times, but they now own a big, two-storey house and are open seven days a week. They are out of the original area, though. They think they may hire some street workers, although they say they are strapped for space. They feed as many as sixty women a day. They have a huge problem with psychiatric care; many sick women have been left with few resources, as has happened in Vancouver.

The nuns have four facilities now, one of them for battered women. Since I left, people continued to work really hard to prove there were homeless women, and to give services to them.

I rang the bell at the convent, determined to find Soeur Georgette Leduc. When we met, we just cried and hugged each other. She is 78 now. She introduced me around as Sheila, the one who started Maison Marguerite. Soeur Georgette now works in the museum. Of course I visited the basement for a talk with Marguerite and more requests. I came back to Vancouver with a sense of home, as if I had been home. My roots were there in Montreal, with the homeless women who now had shelter.

And I give credit to all the staff and boards of Chez Doris and Maison Marguerite, for the work they have done and that they do with homeless women. It's not just who "starts" shelters that counts; it's the ones who continue the work over the years, days in and days out, with dedication.

Maison Marguerite House

Cette maison est toute nouvelle à Montréal. Elle est née d'un appel pressant du Comité des "Femmes sans Abri" fait aux Soeurs Grises de Montréal, en novembre 1976.

Dès 1974, une étude préliminaire fut entreprise sur les refuges possibles pour les femmes alcooliques, itinérantes, de la métropole. Les données indiquèrent clairement qu'il existait un grand besoin pour de tels refuges.

En janvier 1975, un comité composé de représentants intéressés des églises, de groups communautaires et d'agences sociales fut formé dans le but d'offrir à ces femmes en détresse, un gîte temporaire.

Alors, après avoir travaillé sans succès durant près de deux ans, Sheila Baxter, Phylis Davies et Aileen Ross, représentantes du comité, supplièrent les Soeurs Grises de Montréal, d'accepter ce projet des "Femmes sans Abri", "comme Mère d'Youville l'aurait fait."

Les filles de Mère d'Youville ne pouvaient être insensibles à une pareille demande d'offrir un toit, du pain, de l'amitié à ces femmes les plus démunies.

LA MAISON MARGUERITE HOUSE ETAIT FONDÉE!

Annual Statistics
from Chez Doris Annual Report 1989-1990

Month	# of women	French	English	Inuit	Other
April	935	528	326	58	23
May	1,019	526	338	51	104
June	1,001	496	286	127	92
July	863	464	234	86	79
August	1,208	724	314	102	68
Sept.	819	501	186	74	58
October	885	496	219	81	89
November	1,092	612	273	98	109
December	848	458	229	76	85
January	961	518	260	87	96
February	988	542	200	70	176
March	1,123	666	218	64	175
TOTAL	**11,742**	**6,531**	**3,083**	**974**	**1,154**

Percent by age:

18-35   38%
35-55   40%
55+   22%

average women/day: 34
average telephone calls/month: 586
average number of new women/month: 15

(A board member for Chez Doris told me that there is a sharp increase in Inuit homeless people. There is a real need for a social worker who is Inuit.)

* * *

At the Pro-Canada Network conference, I met a professor from a large university. He said he was thinking of writing a book on the corporate agenda. I said, "Great—I'd like to read it, but make sure it's in easy-to-read English."

He replied, "Then I'd have to write *two* books."

I was amazed at this classist statement. If everyone could read the one book, why would he have to write the same book for his fellow academics in 20-syllable words? Is this academic bilingualism? Is it really needed?

I have always wanted to interview a corporate executive. On the plane flying home, a man with shiny black shoes and shiny black socks, sat across from me. He had a shiny red face, and his short hair showed his shiny red ears. The plane had been delayed three hours. It was packed and noisy, and tired babies cried. We talked about plane delays. It turned out that he had tried to get first class, but it was full. He said he was an executive in sales in a large corporation. I said I was a writer and mentioned the conference. Then war broke out—class war.

He: Canada is being drained by free loaders, welfare, U.I., etc. etc. When I first got married I had plastic curtains, now I'm worth millions, he bragged. People are lazy, lazy.

I responded with remarks about corporate greed, homelessness, pollution caused by profit, etc.

He prepared for attack. His ears became more red. "What is your income?" he asked.

"$6000 a year," I replied.

His lips curled back. "You have a free ride, eh? Don't pay taxes, eh? *You're a free rider.*"

I responded with my sweet grandmother look. "No dear, the corporations are the free riders. You take our minerals and resources; you pollute our land for profit; you pay few corporate taxes. What are you going to leave your children? Money and a dying planet?"

"Free rider" echoed through my mind. So I know now what they think; unless you make money for them, you don't deserve to exist. He didn't care what kind of a person I was; he just judged me by my income. His last comment was, if homeless people won't work, they should be left on the street.

* * *

What I learned about the corporate agenda for the homeless: there isn't one. They just don't care. Nothing must stand in the way of profit. People don't count; profit does. They really don't give a damn about homeless people unless the community and the media gets on their case, and then they make token gestures.

Toronto: A Few Facts About Housing and Homelessness

- There are approximately 25,000 homeless persons in Metro Toronto (source: Peter Smith, Peel Housing Commissioner; chair, 1987 International Year of Shelter for the Homeless Canadian Conference)
- In the decade up to 1985, the City of Toronto lost more than 17,000 housing units to gentrification (source: City of Toronto Planning Department)
- Across Ontario, between 15 and 26 affordable rooming house units have been lost *every day* (source: Ontario Task Force on Roomers, Boarders and Lodgers)
- Homelessness kills: a national study shows lower income people die on average six years earlier than upper income people (source: Health and Welfare Canada)
- Homelessness maims: a national study shows lower income people suffer on average at least 14 more seriously disabled years than upper income people (source: Health and Welfare Canada)
- The homeless suffer a crippling amount of disease, including respiratory, skin, and environmentally linked mental disorders (source: Inquiry into the Effects of Homelessness on Health)
- Over the past year, the Ontario Ministry of Housing spent approximately one percent of the overall provincial budget, and only one-third of one percent of the overall budget actually went to new housing
- Under its major non-profit affordable housing program, the Ontario government allocates approximately 2000 new units to Toronto annually. Other programs account for a few hundred additional units, at most (source: industry estimates)
- From July 1987 to June 1988, 25,316 people were served by the

- emergency shelters in Metro Toronto; 15,194 were men, 6,291 were women, and 3,831 were children.
    from BASIC Poverty Action Group, Toronto

No reliable and accurate count of homeless people in Canada currently exists... Prior to the findings of the *National Inquiry on Homelessness* by the Canadian Council on Social Development in September 1987, it was generally suggested that there were between 20,000 and 40,000 homeless people across Canada. These figures were based on estimates derived from studies of the use of emergency shelters and soup kitchens, and generally correspond to those who have been classified as 'street people.'

The CCSD generally agreed with this estimate, although their first report in 1986 defined homelessness as being synonymous with poverty, and evidence was produced indicating that there were over 4.5 million people in Canada living in poverty. When the results of the *National Inquiry on Homelessness* were released, the estimate had been revised to either 100,000 (the number of beds provided to the homeless and destitute during 1986), or between 130,000 and 250,000 (those who do not have secure homes and those whose housing is grossly inadequate).
    from "Homelessness and the Homeless" by H. Peter Oberlander and Arthur L. Fallick

United States

The central question emerging from all this is: What does a society owe to its members in trouble, and *how* is that debt to be paid?

A society owes its members whatever it takes for them to regain their places in the social order... The necessary underlying ethical notion we seem in this nation unable to grasp: that those who are the inevitable casualties of modern industrial capitalism and the free market system are entitled, by right, and by the simple virtue of their participation in that system, to whatever help they need. They are entitled to help to find and hold their places in the society whose social contract they have, in effect, signed and observed.

In any shelter these days you can find men and women who have worked ten, twenty, forty years, and whose lives have nonetheless come to nothing. These are people who cannot afford a place in the world they helped create. And in return? Is it life on the street they have earned? or the cruel charity we so grudgingly grant them?
from "Helping and Hating the Homeless" by Peter Marin, Harper's, January 1990

There are approximately 3 million people homeless in the States. Rents and living expenses are out of reach. Wages are often so low that whole families have to stay in shelters because they don't earn enough to afford rent.

The United States has cut back on social services, and on services to the mentally sick. The U.S. spends billions of dollars on the armed forces and on weapons, but doesn't deal with homelessness. The governments give priority to profit and the marketplace, and do not have the political will to find solutions to homelessness. A government that serves the marketplace at the expense of our environment, our children, our rights to food and shelter, our existence, guarantees that homelessness will increase.

Hunger and homelessness in the U.S.

During 1989, requests for emergency shelter increased overall by an average of 25 percent in the 27 survey cities. About 22 percent of the requests for emergency shelter go unmet.

Seventy-eight percent of cities surveyed said shelters turn away homeless people because of lack of resources. At least 24 percent of homeless families were turned away.

Causes of homelessness are the lack of affordable housing, unemployment and other employment-related problems, mental health problems, substance abuse, lack of services, and poverty.

Consequences of homelessness include: emotional and mental health problems, school-related problems, health problems or inadequate health care, loss of self-esteem and hopelessness, and family problems.

On average, the cities' homeless population is 46 percent

single men, 36 percent families with children, 14 percent single women, 4 percent youth. One in every four homeless persons is a child. Fifty-one percent is black, 35 percent white, and 14 percent members of other races or ethnic groups.

Among homeless families, 79 percent are headed by a single parent. Approximately 24 percent of the requests for shelter from homeless families went unmet. Waiting lists for assisted housing had been closed in two out of three of the surveyed cities.

Shelter and services are particularly lacking for the mentally ill and for families with children.

Twenty-four percent or more of the homeless population is employed in full or part-time jobs.

Eighty-nine percent of the cities expect emergency assistance to increase in 1990. With the decline in federally assisted housing programs, none of the survey cities expect to be able to meet the housing needs of low income people for the foreseeable future.

Charleston
A 21-year-old mother of four, pregnant, has lived with different relatives in the past 5 years. She's on the waiting list for public housing. The relatives were living in condemned housing. She and her four children have been living in a shelter for four months.

Los Angeles
Approximately 1800 homeless are turned away each day because of funding cutbacks. Two shelters have cut back child care services. There is little hope at this time that there will be a positive effect in the near future.

Kansas City
One major group is young people, 15 to 18 years old. Shelters are afraid of liability, and the youth wind up on the street and become targets for pimps and pushers.

Los Angeles
Paul was on the streets with his 15 and 17-year-old sons...yet he was a graduate of two leading European universities and a concert pianist. The family was helped by a

local church that provided temporary housing and aid in their legal problems. Now Paul is working, the children are in school, and they have their own apartment.

Seattle

Those who cannot be served sleep on the street. Youths prostitute themselves in order to secure a place.

Boston

Budget cuts, dismantled mental health system, inaccessible rental housing have lengthened homelessness for many families. The federal government's disinvestment in housing has made the "at risk" people sure of becoming homeless.

Chicago

No significant improvement in the economic status of the city's poor; no increase in low income housing.

Portland

With market rents rising, some of the 71,000 low income households in our community are at risk of becoming homeless. If a family of any size spent all of a welfare check

on rent, they still could not cover median rent in Portland.
   from A Status Report on Hunger and Homelessness in
   American Cities: 1989

Estimates place the number of homeless at between 2 and 3 million. Over one-third of these are mental patients set free under a longstanding program of institutional releases... A 1987 study by the Neighborhood Reinvestment Corporation concludes that as many as 18.7 million low-income Americans may lose affordable housing by the year 2003.

Urban development was responsible for the loss of about 1 million affordable rooms between 1970 and 1980, nearly one-half the total available.

Critics point out that Reagan's plan to provide $200 million in low-income rental housing vouchers is an insignificant amount compared to the $42.8 billion subsidy received by the middle class and rich in the form of home-mortgage tax deductions.
   from "Poverty in America," *Alan Wilson and Elaine Briere,*
   Briarpatch, *April 1988*

I sent a letter to Mitch Snyder, advocate for the homeless in Washington, D.C. and head of the Community for Creative Non-Violence. The letter came back. Before I had a chance to remail it, he died. I would have liked to have talked to him about his work organizing the homeless in the States.

According to a small article in the local newspaper, he hanged himself. He died days after city council voted to stop the 1984 law which guaranteed emergency shelter for everyone in need.

Habitat has reported that one hundred million people have no shelter of any kind, and one billion people—fully one quarter of the world's population—are seriously at risk of becoming homeless because of inadequate shelter and living conditions.

About half the people living in Third World cities have no secure home.

In Yaounde, Cameroon, 80 percent of the people live in illegal squatter settlements.

In Bombay, India, between 100,000 and 500,000 people live on the pavements.

In Mexico City, 60 percent of the population lives in illegal shanty towns.

Meanwhile, in the West, fortunes can be made by the few who can play the property market.

The world's most expensive piece of land for development is in central Ginza district of Tokyo, Japan, where the site of the Crown nightclub was bought for $20,915 per square foot.

The highest rents in the world for prime sites are paid in Manhattan, New York, at $68 per square foot, and London, England, at $51 per square foot—but with service charges and rates, London is top at $87.

from The New Internationalist Calendar, *1989*

In the space of just 15 years, or about 5500 days, the developing world will have to increase by about 65 percent its capacity to produce and manage its urban infrastructure, services, and shelter, merely to maintain present conditions.

from Our Common Future *(the Brundtland report), 1987*

June

A few months ago, a young man of about 18 came to contribute to some poetry readings at Carnegie. He was from Quebec. He had white-blonde hair, dressed in black, presented a proud, confident personality. He wrote and read about a world of tomorrow, where everyone would have enough and there would be peace. When he read he looked like one of those old paintings of an angel. He was a punk angel I guess. He was always hungry and would eat any free food that was around. He was really skinny.

A month later, when he was leaving town, he came to say goodbye. I gave him a hug. It was only then I learned he was homeless and had been living under the viaduct.

I felt such a deep sadness when he left; I guess it pressed the strings of my own homelessness. I was about 12... I'd stay out on the street to avoid the abuse that was waiting for me at home. Dark night hours spent alone, walking the streets, nowhere to go, looking into brightly lit windows where people seemed happy and safe. Children playing, people smiling. My tears would mess up my seeing and I would move on. I wanted a safe warm home too, and people to love me. I sure as hell didn't have one! I found a bench behind a tree in the park, a huge, spreading tree. I tried to sleep. I was scared, but the thought of going back to the abuse was worse, so I stayed till daybreak. I was an expert on survival.

I had coffee with a tall young man in his thirties. He was homeless and had been in prison. "How the hell can you get a job when you don't have an address?" He said his clothes and possessions were scattered. Sometimes he slept on somebody's couch, on the street, and other places where the homeless go to survive. He'd had welfare problems; he'd been robbed of his welfare money the month before, and nobody believed him, so he couldn't pay the hotel. He couldn't get a job. I asked him how he stayed out of trouble. His response: "It's fucking hard. When you see that cash register and you have nowhere to sleep and nothing to eat..." He thought about the cash register as an option. He was pissed off, angry, as he wrapped his six-foot frame around the chair. He couldn't find a way out. A place to stay, with meals, for a month would have helped, perhaps. I didn't ask him too much about his life and personal stuff. He wouldn't have told me anyway. I appreciated the short interview he gave.

I saw today a man in his twenties. He has a disability that leaves him with a limp. He was a hard-working volunteer with a really good education, most of which he got in prison. He had been out for about two months and was seriously trying to get his life together. He looked stressed and tired, but still gave me a hug. Picking up on his sadness, I asked what was wrong. "I've been living on the street for two weeks, that's what's wrong," he said angrily. "I'm going to welfare now. I've got an appointment." He was obviously preparing for battle. I told him I was writing a book on the homeless and asked if I could interview him. "Sure thing," he replied, "later." I wondered if I would see him again.

I had a conversation with a man who is about 40. He told me he had cashed his U.I. cheque and got rolled for his money. He had no choice but to live on the street. He survived by putting on a turtleneck sweater, carrying some books so he looked like a student. Then he would sleep at UBC during the daytime with a book over his face. At night he stayed awake on the street. I admired his survival instincts and his sense of humour.

If you are on a week-to-week income, any crisis that takes money can put you on the street. Low-income workers don't make enough to save money. No money, out you go!

Jodie

When someone from the community dies that we know, we get together in the Carnegie Theatre. We put out a white tablecloth with candles and flowers; we serve cake and coffee. Once, when it was during a cold spell, we even had beef stew.

One by one we stand up as we choose and talk about the person who has died. Members do not pass unnoticed.

It's a moving and beautiful experience, one of solidarity, and a time to grieve. So it was for Jodie, who had recently chosen to die by suicide. We had known her for many years. Each person who spoke had a different part of her to relate.

Jodie had a social worker and friend who said that one of Jodie's worst fears was having to move back into a hotel room again.

Jodie had a history of mental illness. She had been doing much better these past years. She had an apartment in the east end. When I saw her once in a while, she would say "hi" in passing. Jodie had a relapse and had to go into hospital for a few months. I don't know the details; I just know that when she came out of hospital, her apartment was no longer available for her. The rent had increased drastically, and welfare rental allowance is $275 a month. All she could rent was a hotel room.

Marilyn, Jodie's social worker friend, said poverty contributed to Jodie's death. If she had had enough money to start up a home again, she wouldn't have chosen to die. When I interviewed Ralph Buckley at Strathcona Community Health Team, he said many of his clients that were ill were living in these hotels.

Living in a hotel means living in a small room with a window, a bed, a table, and two chairs, a toilet down the hall, a flimsy lock, roaches, noise. Many people die unnoticed; homeless people don't make the media pages when they die.

We said goodbye to Jodie, but I feel anger, rage: this is unfinished business. Pulling these hotels down without replacing them with low-rental homes makes the situation worse.

Alan Redway, Minister of State for Housing

On June 26, 1990, Alan Redway, the federal Minister of State for Housing, gave a press conference to media and social housing tenants to announce that $3.2 million was going to be spent to support greater participation by residents in public housing.

My constant insecurity is that the government will sell or bulldoze the public housing I live in. For some reason, I have no faith in the government because I know the land where I live is very valuable, and it's been my experience that what corporations want, they take. And I believe, mistakenly or not, that corporations and government are one and the same. Anyway, I asked these questions:

What are you doing about the homeless crisis? I live here with my cat. I'm very happy here. I want to stay. Can you give me a guarantee that these properties won't be sold and bulldozed?

His response:

"What I would say about a guarantee about what's going to happen here specifically is the consultation process that I referred to will take place before anything might occur and that's not to say anything will be occurring or anything else."

That's double talk!

"I hope not, I hope not. I don't want to give you the impression, for instance, that the world will not change at any time...I can't give you that absolute guarantee. At the same time I can't tell you that the world *will* change. But if there is at any time some thought that there would be some changes here, you and all of those that live here certainly will be involved fully in the process of discussing what might happen. But that's not to say that anything will happen.

"However, in the consultation process that is going on now in public housing, and the valuation process that we have just undertaken, we have found that many of the projects across the country are getting older, and need some major work done on them, so obviously we've got to take that into account. I can't tell you right off the top of my head what the situation is here. I did hear there are some difficulties with some of the aspects of the units. I guess actually it wasn't here, was it? It was another project so...it may be that everything's fine and dandy here, and if that's the case, obviously things will continue to go on.

But if there is any thought at any time of doing anything in the way of a change here, you certainly will be part of that process. It isn't going to be that you're going to wake up tomorrow and find yourself out on the street.

"Now, on your other aspect of the homeless, I share the concern that you have expressed. People right across the country have expressed their concerns about homeless people. We've got to do as much as we can and more than we are doing. You can appreciate the difficult problems there are to find the wherewithal. What we are trying to do is to make the most of what we have and to try and find some innovative ways to do things even better than they are, and any thoughts that you have with respect to that or any thoughts that anyone in any other housing project, is one that I welcome because I sure don't have all the answers. I'm looking for them and I know that there's a lot of good thoughts and good ideas out there. I need your help."

Karen Gallagher, YWCA Hotel

I went to interview Karen at the YWCA Hotel on Burrard. It was raining really hard. I was full of apprehension, and arrived early. I went downstairs to the cafeteria with its yellow, uncheerful walls. It had not changed much. The hotel above seemed more touristy, though.

Memories came flooding back. I had stayed here after the fire in 1980, until they had evicted me and my daughters because I couldn't pay. I should have felt anger. Instead I felt pain, guilt, frustration, and fear.

I was honest with Karen, and told her of my past experiences. She said, "I wouldn't have evicted you, that's for sure." She told me about her job, and what happens now when women have to stay at the Y.

"I am the director of the housing services department, which is a new department. It's been in place for seven months. I manage the hotel and have ultimate managing responsibilities for the Vancouver Housing Registry. As well, we are looking at developing affordable social housing for women and children in need in Vancouver.

"I come from an advocacy position in the way that I do my work. That's how I try to structure the policies in the hotel residence. We still get refugee women throughout the year, women in emergency situations. There are some people we can't house here because of their specific needs, women who need a level of care that we cannot provide. If someone was actively psychotic and acting out, and they were dangerous to themselves or somebody else, this is not an appropriate building for someone like that.

"The women that show up looking for housing mostly are mature, single women over 40. Some of them have life-skills difficulties, can't work, or they are the working poor, or are on some kind of disability pension. There's nothing available in their price range unless you want to go into some hotel where you don't feel safe as a woman alone. It's not appropriate for your need so it doesn't feel like a home. I believe very strongly that people have a right to feel that their house is a home. If you don't have that, you don't have a whole lot.

"Basically, there's not a whole lot out there that we can make referrals to, and we scramble like mad. With the vacancy rate the way it is, and the demolition that's going on, it's extremely difficult to get adequate housing for people. We're not talking about fancy housing, we're talking about a real basic, clean, safe place to stay and to live so that you can feel that it's your home."

I've been told that statistics on homeless women are low because women will use their bodies to get shelter rather than risk the street.

"I think that's really true. I think women are forced to make those kinds of decisions when there are no other options for them.

"It's really frightening for me to think about what happens to those women when they have to make those choices, and I wonder whether women who are disappearing or who are experiencing all kinds of horrible things, is it coming from having to make that choice.

"We have twenty-five women that live here year round in our residence, and I have absolutely no interest in moving them on. This is their home and this is where they will live as long as they choose to."

[Author's note: They pay $300 a month to stay at the Y. Their welfare cheque allows $275 for rent and phone, so I guess the extra $25 would have to come out of their food money.]

What about racism?

"Especially native Indians or anybody of colour are really discriminated against in Vancouver and all of our country really. Once somebody sees that they're native, then all of a sudden the place is already rented. If they think they have a native accent on the phone, they'll say it's already rented. When we try to work with owners around that, they have all kinds of negative stereotypes of who people are, who people of colour are. If they're poor, it's even worse, and if they're on welfare and a single mom—it's like they've got six strikes against them. So it's a real crisis situation for those people.

"At the Vancouver Housing Registry we had a devil of a time finding a house for a native woman with three kids. No landlord wanted to rent to her. She wasn't very high up on the list in B.C. housing, and the native housing has a long waiting list. She came in every day for six weeks, and she was finally able to find housing. I was shocked how incredibly blatant the racism was.

"A lot of transition houses find a real problem moving women on once they've gone through the process you go through; they can't find places out there that are affordable, or they're being discriminated against because they have kids. That means they stay in the transition house for months, when before they would move on after thirty days. That prevents other women who are needing to flee a violent situation from having access, because there are people already there. It's an incredible scenario, and women are being beaten daily, and they can't flee because there's no place for them to go.

"On behalf of some politicians there is [a political will to deal with these problems]. Other people choose to focus on other things. I believe there's some people who think that people who are homeless deserve what they get, that they have done something wrong or they wouldn't wind up in that situation. Some people say they are reaping what they've sown."

"I think there's a broad spectrum where people aren't getting adequate housing and the government does not seem to be showing the desire to work towards good solutions.

"We've had enough task forces and we've had enough discussion about the problem. Let's get real. Let's work together, because people are going to start dying on the street soon if we don't do something now. Not next year—now!"

After I left the YWCA, I walked out to Burrard Street. It was pouring rain. I couldn't see through my glasses and my body soon got soaked. I just walked, remembering painful things that had been deeply buried inside my mind: the pain of leaving my family, the pain of homelessness. I couldn't cry.

I was aware that I went for my usual fix at this time. I don't do drugs or booze, so I had a "hit" of fish and chips and two chocolate bars. It soothed the pain a little. I can understand why homeless people are often substance abusers. They do it to erase the pain. My drug of choice to ease the pain was food.

I turned to close friends and family for comfort. My youngest daughter said, "But look how well we've all turned out. We're together now. Isn't that what counts?"

Next morning it was like the rainbow after the storm. I think I dealt with the situation, faced the hurricane—I'm no longer stuck. I can move on. It's history, healing has begun.

My homelessness as a child and a teenager was survivable, but the guilt feelings of leaving my family because of no choices was, for me, amputation of the mind.

In 1973, Canada's federal housing minister said:

"It is the fundamental right of every Canadian to have access to good housing at a price he can afford. Housing is not simply an economic commodity that can be bought and sold according to the vagaries of the market, but a social right.". . .

There are estimated to be 800,000 more Canadians living in poverty in the mid 1980s than there were in the late 1970s. . . .

Canadian Mortgage and Housing estimated, in the early 1980s, that over 500,000 renter households could not afford adequate accommodation, and nearly 200,000 homeowners had serious problems affording their housing. . . .

In 1985, the federal government released three major housing policy documents:
- *Consultation Paper on Housing* (January)
- *Housing Programs in Search of Balance* (June)
- *A National Direction for Housing Solutions* (December)

The words "homeless" and "homelessness" can not be found in any of these reports.

> from "Who Are the Homeless? What Is Homelessness?" by David Hulchanski and Arthur L. Fallick.

Emergency Services

I called the provincial government in Victoria, and talked to a person who's in the Ministry of Social Services and Housing. She told me that no one needs to be without shelter; they just have to

JUNE

call the Emergency Services branch of MSSH. She said if anyone is without shelter, it's because they choose to be.

I tried to talk to her about the problems the community groups have finding low-rental accommodation for people, and asked her what happens if people don't qualify for help. She said she would mail me some literature. She didn't listen too well. In fact, she was hostile.

I asked her to explain to me the "charter," some kind of agreement between the province and the city that has to do with housing, building laws, etc. She told me that was a municipal affair and I should talk to the mayor. She was not prepared to discuss it. All she said was, "The mayors want to make their charters more palatable." I asked her to whom. She got mad and said she wouldn't discuss it.

I talked to an old friend who has worked at Carnegie Centre. He told me shelterless people would approach him for help. The process he followed was, if they were functioning, he would give them the number of Emergency Services. If they were not, which was often the case, he would try to make a referral by calling Emergency Services.

The lines were always busy. They put you on hold. They would say they would call back and not return the call.

The big problem is that you can't go to Emergency Services as before; now there is only phone contact. He said, as a front-line worker, he had been totally frustrated. Most often he didn't get called back, so when he left he would just pass the number over to the homeless person. He said there was too much red tape and that he seldom had success with them.

I spoke to a director of a community drop-in. She said, "You've got to be persistent. You've got to be pushy when dealing with E.S." That's how she managed, but she felt anyone that wasn't persistent would easily fall through the cracks.

Karen Howe, an advocate with First United Church, also works at a drop-in that's open till midnight. "We've had women ask us to find a place to stay," she told me. "If they are a quieter nature, non-aggressive, and don't know the ropes, then they are most likely not going to get the service they should be getting."

Karen had several criticisms of E.S. "One, if you don't have access to a free phone, you have to come up with the money to make the phone calls. When you call Emergency Services, most often you're told to phone the different hostels in the area to find out what's available and then call back. If you only have one quarter you're s.o.l. That means you would have to walk to these places from wherever you are to find out if there's space there. So once again, the expectations are that, because you are poor, you can suffer, therefore you can walk or do without.

"The circumstances I face, with women coming in—we are looking at most of Vancouver's transition houses being filled by mid-month if not earlier. These women are in need of a safe place to stay, and their only options are places like Lookout or Triage where they may have to deal with the very type of men these women are trying to stay away from. Even there the options that the Emergency Services can provide are very limited. They won't consider putting up a woman in a hotel for an evening, to keep her in her own personal space. They would put her up in Lookout instead.

"The process for Emergency Services, if you're not eligible for welfare, is you have to self-refer. It's a maximum of three nights. You can continue that process because they can't refuse you. The ministry is obligated by the very intent of their act, which is to relieve poverty, neglect, and suffering, to continue to put people up. The problem is that they don't always make that clear to everybody, so people wind up sleeping on the street. They don't know that they are eligible to go there every night. Stay is three days, then you have to see a worker. People get told they have three days max, then you have to find other accommodation. People don't know that, even if they don't qualify for assistance, they have to help you.

"I don't think that it's adequately staffed. Most of the experiences I've had, there are about two workers there at midnight. I couldn't even hazard a guess of how many calls, and they also have to be in touch with the Kiddy Car. It took an hour and a half for it to come for us once."

Liz

Liz is in a shelter right now. Her two sons are in foster care. She is in her late twenties.

"Basically what happened is when I was pregnant with my second child I was staying with a friend and after I had the baby I moved into a place, December 1989. Everything was going well although it was somewhat unaffordable—$600 a month plus half the utilities. It was a three bedroom and really very nice. Then I found out in January that the owner of the place wanted to sell it. He sold it in March 1990. I had two months to find a place, which was very difficult with two small children. I became very stressed because nothing was available. If there was something available it was too expensive, and when you're on assistance you can only afford $514 a month, which includes utilities and your telephone. Most places are $600 or more for two or three bedrooms. I don't have that kind of money or resources. The other alternative is finding someone who will share accommodation with me. You have to be sure that the personalities click.

"My kids are in care now because I'm really very stressed out. I just couldn't handle things anymore, and I'm staying in a recovery house right now.

"My definition of homelessness is when you are not in a place that you can feel secure, that you can be with your children. Solutions to homelessness? Affordable housing that is geared to what your income is. Another solution would be for every city to have a moratorium on demolition so that affordable housing is not destroyed and also welfare rates should be raised so people can live."

July

It's mid-July. Amazingly the squatters are still on Frances Street, and the squatting movement seems to be growing.

Betty McPhee of Crabtree says there are even more homeless now. Most workers tell me the problems are increasing. Georgina Marshall, an advocate employed by First United Church, was concerned that distressed people in need of shelter need to talk to a face, a person they can see, not a voice on the phone. People in crisis and stress need a location to go to, to get assistance in finding a shelter.

Because Emergency Services are done by phone, it keeps the homeless invisible, keeps the statistics lower, because you have to be well to call, call back, call hotels, and find a way of getting there. This has been said many times. My apologies for repeating it, but this is reality, not entertainment. Poverty, homelessness, addictions, depression, hunger, lice, and surviving is boring—same thing day in, day out...sandwich and soup lines...a stale sub from a dumpster..."Move on. Don't sleep here"...panhandle some change, buy a bottle to dull the pain...wait to die.

Ada

It was about 9 p.m. I was sitting on the bench at Main and Hastings, waiting for the bus to go home. A tall, older woman, about 70, sat down beside me. She had several layers of clothing on, her face and hands showed that deep brown and leather look of someone that spends much time outside. I started a conversation with her.

She said, "I'm on my way to Arizona. I hear the swimming is good there." I said it was good here too.

Ada had come to B.C. in the early 1970s with her husband. They had lived in Nova Scotia. Her husband died shortly after they arrived here. She said she was very depressed and lonely. Sometimes she lived in a room, but she didn't like the people around her. Ada wanted to go to Arizona because that was the plan she and her husband had had.

"I go every day to the missions. I spend all my time in missions. If it wasn't for missions, I would be lonely, but I'm going to Arizona. I want to swim there." She had huge brown spots on her sun-browned hands. Her eyes were a kind of cornflower blue. They watered. I wasn't sure if it was tears or just aging. I told her about the book I was writing, and asked her why there were homeless people and what could be done about it.

"It's all in the Bible. It's all been prophesied. It's all in the Bible. Read the prophecies. It's all there. But I'm going to Arizona."

My bus came. She stayed on the seat and we said goodbye. She could be anyone's grandmother. There she was, lonely, obviously sleeping out, and still grieving her dead husband. The comfort the mission gave her was obvious. It's not my choice, but she had a right to hers.

Owl House

Owl House is on a beautiful tree-lined street, a big old house, with stained glass windows. It was very different from the Hastings hotels where I had interviewed people.

Owl House is an emergency temporary shelter specializing in the needs of natives. It is unique because it takes fathers as well as mothers and kids. No single men but sometimes single women. No active substance abusers are admitted. They have a limit of fifteen people. Most are from Ministry of Social Services and Housing referrals. MSSH pays for their clients. There are three spots for outside referrals, but they have to be paid for from somewhere. Two years ago they were not at full capacity; now they turn away at least a hundred requests a week. The majority of the staff are native. They are understaffed and underpaid, the director said. They all earn less than eight dollars an hour. They have a very limited transport allowance, and no vehicle to take their clients to appointments, or to look for housing.

I had lunch with the moms and the kids on a large wooden table. We talked.

One non-native woman with a native Indian husband told me that when she phones for accommodation, landlords ask, "What's your ethnic background?" When she tells them she is Russian Ukrainian and her husband is a Cree Indian, they slam the phone down on her. The women said, "Not only do landlords refuse children, they refuse us because we're native."

A native woman and a white woman who are friends went to look at a house. The native woman knocked on the door. The door was opened, she was told, "It's taken," and the door was slammed in her face. The white woman waited a little while, then went up and knocked on the door. The door was opened and she was invited in to look at the still-vacant apartment. I asked if anyone reported them. I was told no, because natives complaining are often not taken seriously by authorities, unless they're in a position of power and it's political.

People are in the shelter for different reasons. There are battered women, homeless families, and sometimes teenagers over sixteen—under sixteen they have to be with an adult. One woman was there with three very small children, recovering from an abusive situation. I asked her what was happening. She said she couldn't look for a place yet, she was too stressed out, so she would be transferred, perhaps to a transition house. She had beautiful healthy children who clung to her as she tried to feed the baby. Another woman was there with a premature baby that had breathing problems. She had left an abusive relationship. One of the problems women face is that they and their children leave and the abuser has the apartment.

Emily, homeless with one baby, told me, "The $465 from welfare for rent and Hydro and phone just isn't enough. The landlords don't want children and when I go there and they see me they say the place is rented. Homelessness is scary... no sense of security. Social workers make you feel like a piece of shit. This housing is ridiculous. But I'll keep looking. I want to move out of here. I don't want to depend on anybody."

It took time for Emily to speak. A lot of the time her thoughts were spoken slowly, with obvious pain as she remembered the doors slammed in her face by landlords because she was native, a single mother, and on welfare. "The reason I'm homeless is because I was staying with a friend and she moved out and I had no choice. I didn't want to bring the baby down to one of those hotels on Hastings. I don't want to stay here. But I have no choice."

Another woman said, "Homelessness is not being treated fair. Feels like you're on the low level of nothing. People look down on you. Like social workers put you under a pile of paperwork and forget you. They just want you to disappear, like forget you, you're just a piece of paper, put us under a pile on the desk and forget us."

She was young, about 23, happy because she had just had her two-year-old son returned to her. Her other child was in hospital and would be there for a while. She was also seven months pregnant. She and her native husband had come to Vancouver from back east. His job didn't happen. The four of them had been put in various emergency accommodations. The last month, while waiting for their welfare cheque to be processed, they were leaving to go back east in her van when they were stopped and pulled over. The authorities thought they were living in the van. (She said this was because they had a dog, and there was dog shit in the back of the van.) The kids were apprehended and she had just got her son back. They were staying at Owl House and she said her husband had been arrested on very serious charges.

She wants to find a three-bedroom apartment or house, because there will be three kids when the next one is born. She said, "I missed my child so much when he was apprehended. I'm so glad to get him back. Then the other may be home in months. I have never been separated from my children before. This has been a wicked month for me. My van was impounded because I had no insurance." She said the most important choice for her was finding a home for her and her children. She said before, when she had gone house-hunting with her husband, they had run into problems because she and her children are white and her husband is native.

Another woman said, "If I don't go back to him I haven't even got a spoon. He has everything. I have nothing; it's all his. We're not married or anything."

Cheryl Janzen, the director of Owl House, said that the vacancy rate is a white statistic. "The non-white vacancy rate is much narrower. The racial myth that all natives are involved in unproductiveness and alcohol is not true. The Indian Act destroyed the natives' right to community access, while securing the right to vote and get a trade paper. You had to give up your status in exchange for a university degree or a trade paper. The Indian Act destroyed livelihoods. For example, native fishermen were given limited access to fishing rights on the Fraser, to the economic advantage of the non-native, so this generation is faced with the task of recovery on top of the racism and ignorance. The bottom line is we have native visibility in the downtown eastside. Because of their economic status it's cheaper to house them there than in decent hotels."

The women talked about how hard it was to get bus fare from their workers to look for housing. Cheryl Janzen said that women can not just sit around; they have to go out and look for accommodation or they're moved out. I asked her where. She said to another shelter. I was aware of how tired the women looked, and the feeling they had of being treated as a piece of shit by the society that blames them. Powerlessness was being reinforced by the blaming of the victim.

August

A tent city outside the Vancouver Art Museum grows with supporters of the Mohawks at Oka. I counted over 50 tents. People are camping on the lawns; the water fountain is a source of constant attraction for small children living in the tents. A huge canvas covers the steps at the entrance to the grounds. People have organised a kitchen. A 40-gallon drum holds a fire, people sit around, and a drum beats softly. Passers-by on Georgia stare as they shop at the big stores or go to work in the high-rise offices around the park.

A woman from the group brought two young people to Carnegie. They were homeless. They were both 17, from Ontario; he was native and she was non-native. The person who brought them for help was concerned because they were underage, homeless, had no money and no ID. The staff person in the learning centre asked me to help.

The young woman wanted nothing to do with Family Services; the young man was very sick with a high fever, and could scarcely sit up. I called DEYAS, and they told me to bring the two over. On the way, I stopped off at the street nurse to see if she could help the man.

The problem of underaged kids with no ID, or runaways from group homes, foster homes, abusive homes, is very difficult. They can't go to the authorities because they are scared of being shipped back to the places they ran from. So many underaged kids live on the street because of these kinds of circumstances.

I don't know what happened to these two; I was just a vehicle to get them to the people who would try to help them.

* * *

She was a tiny woman who looked like a hippy from the 1960s. She was staying in a tent, supporting the Mohawks, at the art museum. She told me the problem poor renters were facing on Saltspring Island. Rentals had climbed sky high; Saltspring had become trendy. The house she was renting was sold. She couldn't find another rental cheap enough, so she stayed with friends for a while until it was just too much. She then moved into a tent with her three children and lived there for three months. She was going back, determined to stay on Saltspring, even in a tent if she has to.

Melissa

What's it like living on the street?

"Afraid, lonely, no one seems to care. You ask someone for a cup of coffee; they put their nose up in the air and walk away like you're a piece of crumb. No one wants to associate with you. They think you're all bad. You feel very isolated.

"When I came back to Vancouver I wasn't able to get a place. I wasn't able to get financial assistance till I found a place. So I had to either stay in a hostel—and I won't stay in a hostel—so I stayed out on the street.

"You gotta keep one eye open and one eye closed...sitting there...keep an eye all around you. Keep your eyes open all the time, watching every move, cos you don't know what's gonna pop behind you or how they are gonna react to you. There's a lot of sexual, like, people coming up and asking you for sex, or having smart remarks. I was raped about a month ago. I'm still going through it, and I'm going through it alone.

"So people start opening their god-darn eyes, start looking around them and see there's people much worse off than them, and have a little more consideration and kindness in their heart, maybe there won't be so many lonely people. If people took time and interest in homeless people. I can't really say about everybody, but they are still human beings. I don't care who they are, they still need someone to take care of them, have interest in them, and help them get off the street. Show that there's something for them to do instead of staying on the street. That there's people there to care and take interest."

Danyeh

"Homelessness for me is always having to depend on social assistance and not being able to express myself to others—such as social workers/doctors/etc.—and always trying to prove myself worthy. I am worthy to myself and children, but to prove to others that I am, I seem to have to make a scene, such as yelling or act impatient and demanding. So what if people look at me and I put myself in an embarrassing situation, and humiliate myself? To try and express to get my needs met? I feel that social assistance governors can't even get their shit together as well as their stress levels. How can people in this line of work tell me how to live when they have more problems trying to shuffle their employees around or half of them quit because of stress-related problems themselves? I would rather sleep in a tent in the open of nature and teach my children their schooling by correspondence; they'd end up knowing about life. So what if it's on the streets—it would learn them the truth about what this world is really like because living in a home and having to depend on welfare and getting your children off to school each morning, wondering what they're coming home to is a worry on them. If we were to live openly, at least my children can learn independence and respect, not only for themselves, but for others doing the same thing. Welfare employees are stressed out and take it out on innocent victims, some of which really are trying. We have feeling on this side of the counter, too. I also feel there's too many superiors under the cloak of justice. Power-tripping policemen and people just too busy on what they're doing to even care about others. Living on the streets seems more safer knowing there are people, anyone sometimes, that care and really care about you instead of a false smile and phony hugs from burnt-out people wanting and needing them themselves."

Margaret Anderson, Evelyne Saller Centre

I went in to the Evelyne Saller Centre (also known as the Alex, or the 44) to talk to Margaret Anderson. She works in a small dark office at the back of the centre, where people come to get a shower, do their laundry, or have their lice removed. There were so many people sitting around... numbers were called when it was a person's turn. This was no fancy office with leather chairs and plants, like social workers have. I realize that the people who do the front-line work have very poor working conditions, yet the government experts with their 9 to 4, Monday to Friday, have comfortable surroundings to work out of.

"My definition of homeless is anybody without a door to shut, to call their own. That's my basic definition. It's been broken down into people who are shelterless, people who are living in emergency accommodation, people who are living on the street. But to me it's anybody without a door of their own to shut.

"Homelessness is on the increase. I have worked in this community many years. It's becoming sort of a canker. Before, some people would sleep out voluntarily, to save their shelter portion or whatever. It's not voluntary anymore. There's more and more doing it because they just don't have a choice. I live in Kits, which is a fair distance from here, and they're over there now. They're in Stanley Park, Wreck Beach, all over.

"It's still a low ratio for women. They probably make up five to eight percent of our population. For homeless women, the options, I hesitate to say, are slightly better. They can always find a place to sleep, even if it means sometimes using her body in exchange.

"Most of our clients that we talk to on a daily basis [are homeless]. I can't give you an exact quote, but at least a third of our population [users of the centre] are living in cars, living under the viaduct, living on floors, etc. It's a mixture of people. It's hardcore alcoholic that's traditionally associated with this community, there's quite a few of them. There's the fairly new homeless. They cannot find another place to move to. They've been turfed out of their rooms, or when they close down hotels, some guys don't even try any more.

"I know a guy who's been living in the back seat of his car for three months now with his dogs. He just can not find a place that he can afford. I can think of a woman right now, with three kids under the age of three, who's living in a place that you wouldn't keep cows in, and she's paying over $600. By the time she pays her utilities, she's paying $700. No hot water half the time, half the time the plumbing isn't going, no heat half the winter, splintering floors, filth and garbage. There's more kids on the skids than I've ever seen before. I'm talking about children, not teens on the loose. I'm talking about families with babies. They're staying at the skid row hotels more than I've ever seen down here before.

"They have lost what housing they've got. They could have come in from out of town. They can't find anything that they can humanly afford, and a lot of places won't take children. They may go to welfare and Emergency Services will put them in a hotel room. Once they're in that hotel room, they're stuck because they can't find any place to go to. The waiting list for low-cost housing is so long. Forget it.

"[Homeless people are younger]—a lot in their twenties, kids in their teens squatting anywhere there's a vacant building, anywhere they can break into. They come here to bathe, do their laundry, eat. Come here to spend the day, all day sometimes. Then they go back and sleep at the squat.

"I feel that this community is being shovelled under, that its needs are not being looked at, that the attitude is 'the sooner it's cleaned up and cleared out the better.' It doesn't give any fucking regard to the people who have lived here for years, literally years. It doesn't give any regard to the people who are the poorest members of our society, gives them no options. And until any level of

government gets off its bleeping ass and really looks at it as a problem that's going to get way worse, then it's going to just get way worse.

"Solutions—protect what we've got instead of allowing closures. Stop demolitions. Keep buildings upgraded. Some level of government's got to take some responsibility and provide affordable housing. I know they can't house everybody, but they could increase the affordable housing stock. In the case of the mentally ill, there's got to be some better planning before they are released. They're just kicked out into the community now. I don't care what anybody says, it's not adequate. They're being abused physically, they're being abused sexually, they're being abused financially. They're targets period."

But I've been told that there are not too many homeless.

"Maybe you're not talking to people who talk to these people every day. I do. I talked to them every day for ten years. They're not my clients, they're my friends, so it's easy for me to say to them, 'You're doing without? You got a place? Sleeping out?' They tell me, but they won't tell their worker."

Who do you think are the experts on homelessness?

"Besides the homeless? People on the front line, community workers dealing immediately with the clientele, public health people, people running the drop-ins, people running the soup lines, food banks. Anybody who really deals intensely with the people, who are right on the front line. They have the reality. They know. It's those who deal with the same people day in and day out.

"Here, we provide laundry, showers, delousing, and first aid for the residents of the downtown eastside. Actually, we get them from much further away. We do fifty laundries a day, we see over 100 showers a day. We've been doing more delousing, which I attribute to a lot of people being out of shelter because they're packing under the viaduct and it's not sanitary, not clean, and there's no way to get away from it. I have not seen such an increase in lice and scabies as I've seen this year in fourteen years.

"The level of frustration is higher, but a lot of that is the influx of cocaine into the community. The changes in the last two years are phenomenal. More strong-arming, more violence, more unpredictability. Coke coming into the community in a big way—it didn't just infiltrate the community, it avalanched.

"If you can't afford to eat and sleep, you can still afford to prostitute yourself, you can afford to wait in the alley for some old bugger to come reeling out of the bar, bop him over the head and dig into his pockets. They don't even wait till it's dark. They don't even wait for him to come out of the bar, man. You go into the washroom in the bar and you're dead meat. You cannot defend yourself. Ask the police. This has gone up phenomenally. Anything to acquire the money for the addiction. It's not a new trend. It's always been a trend. But the level of it is new."

As I left, there were about 30 or 40 people sitting around. There was a line-up for the lunch that cost a buck and a half. It was packed with all kinds of people needing a cheap meal—the homeless, the people in shelter, the poor. Some hotel rooms have no cooking facilities, so this would be a place for hotel tenants too. Some looked like they hadn't bathed in months. Some talked to themselves. Young, old, eating together. The basic need—food. Not the best place to bring little children, but it's better than letting them starve.

September, October, November

Six months later, the squatters are still on Frances Street. They have kept six houses squatted. The leadership probably has changed a little, and some people have come and gone, but what counts is that they have sent a message, loud and clear, to the developers who kick tenants out, leaving houses vacant for months. I believe the squatters have been given a summons. Whatever happens, to have kept these homes available to people for six months is truly a victory.

I was on the Main Street bus. Pierre was there, squashing his lice, bugging people, laughing insanely. I was reading the *Province*. I tried to avoid eye contact because then he would really act out.

As I got off the bus at Main and Hastings, I offered him my newspaper to read, smiled at him, said "See you." He took the paper. I just wanted to reach out to him, treat him with some dignity, but when someone's so dirty, scratching lice, acting "crazy," it's difficult.

Pablo, DEYAS

Pablo is a street worker with DEYAS. He has a reputation as a good street worker. He also works with refugees, and with children as young as 12, who are homeless and prostitute themselves on the street to keep a roof over their heads. The people Pablo works with are often scared of institutions.

I talked to Pablo in the office behind the needle exchange on Main. It was a busy, noisy place with people, street people, coming and going, mostly young people.

* * *

"My work is to walk on the street, try to find runaway youth. We're trying to take services to street level. We work with intravenous drug users, women who are involved in prostitution, youth that are involved with drug dealing, substance abusers, alcohol abusers, sexually abused... Many of them sleep out in the parks or under the viaduct, or they crash in friends' houses, or sell their body to be able to have a place to sleep or to have a place to eat.

"Our society has put a trick on the people. They're collecting welfare, and with the money that welfare give you, the only way you can rent a place for yourself is to come down to the east area. The downtown eastside is the cheapest in town. You go, you rent a room, the room is a dirty one, it's old, has cockroaches, rats... Only animals live there, and you have to live like an animal. What happens next is, they pay the rent for a month—ten days later the landlord kick them out and rent the room again. According to DERA, 80 to 90 percent of the hotels in the area do that. Or what they do is, when the guy's not there, they kick the door, they trash the place, they take whatever they want, the food, possessions he bought for three weeks with the $193 that he received from welfare. He went and he bought the food and stuff for his next three, four weeks. When he comes back, the food is not there.

"People sleep in the park. In Oppenheimer. What happened is, the park moved the benches away. The police come down and give them a ticket. They charge them with drunkenness, drinking in an open place. They put you a ticket and they make you move.

"It's the same if they're in a hostel, the Catholic charities; they have to be there a certain hour, and at 7 o'clock in the morning they're kicked out again. So then the only place they have to go is to wander on the street. The problem is that a person in that situation probably only sleep an hour and a half, at most two hours. The rest he walks, sits in a coffee shop, he waits."

I asked Pablo about homeless refugees in the community.

"The landlords abuse them. They don't speak much English. They don't expect to be robbed by the landlord. Immigration takes too much time to resolve the paperwork. Without the working permit, the action of waiting creates stress, so the people start to have a drink as some medicine to take part of the pressure out of their system and they end up drinking their cheque, abusing drugs. It's just a vicious circle that they can't run away. They can't resolve their immigration papers. They can't find a job. They don't have a work permit. And when they get their work permit, they can't speak English enough to find a job. They keep waiting and waiting and waiting. We have people out there waiting for four years.

"What many people don't realize is that these are the people that don't have interior strength. They have a rough life. They don't really know how to solve their problems. The language barrier becomes a big wall to cross, and the problem becomes bigger.

"These people are out of the community, are out of society. We have native, Latin, Caucasian. They don't accept services from society. They don't even collect welfare any more. There's too many papers, too many appointments, too many requests. If we want to move these people and incorporate them into society, then we have to bring the services to them. We have to start drug and alcohol counselling groups at street level, and mental health groups at street level. We have to be creative in the way we offer jobs to these people in terms of job readiness programs. We have to create the resources to put these people, and be sure they're going to stay, in the hotels, that they're not going to get kicked out of their hotels. We have to provide for safe housing. Safe doesn't have to mean rich.

"We have a part of the population that accepts places like hostels and christian charities, another part of the population that accepts Lookout. But we have to come up with more innovative services, more innovative home places for these people. The general attitude is, 'I don't like to go to charities, hostels. Even though the service is great, the place is terrible—is like a jail.'

"I think that we have two problems: one is the cutbacks, and the other is the bad use of the services that they have. Meaning they put it for political purposes to win the next election so that instead of giving a good service to the community, the reality is, people don't want to go there. Lousy service. They give money and employment to friends of the politicians instead of leaving it to the community to solve.

"I'm talking about counselling in a bar, counselling in a park, counselling on the sidewalk, just sit on the floor and talk, or you can walk. For the last two years I'm requesting Mental Health Department to send a mental health worker down to the street. Nobody wants to come; they work from offices.

Dugout, on Powell Street, where people drop in for coffee and a visit

"People don't go to offices. They're sick of paperwork, they're sick of appointments. They can't cope with it. They make their appointments at 8 o'clock in the morning. That's a set-up. When I fix an appointment for a street person, I fix it for 2, 3, or 4 o'clock in the afternoon, and on top, I have to go and kick him out of bed and make sure he shows up."

October

It's now well into the fall. The nights are cold, and homeless people sometimes shelter in commercial garbage containers.

A man named Bunnie, in his early thirties, fell asleep or passed out in a garbage container. The container was slowly loaded onto the garbage truck, and the contents were crushed and mangled. Bunnie's body was discovered at the Burnaby incinerator. His body was dangling from the scoop. He was nearly incinerated.

Apparently this isn't the first time this has happened. One official said that it's very sad that our society is unable to cope with the small minority in our community that ends up in this type of situation.

How many homeless will die this winter? How many mentally sick people will be abandoned to live on the street? How many boys/girls/women/men will sell their bodies for a place to sleep? This is most definitely a social problem, not a personal one.

I met a policeman who looked approachable, so I approached him, and asked him what the police did for homeless people who were sleeping out. He said that, unless someone complains, they leave them sleeping. When a person is drunk the police try to get them into detox overnight.

He was genuinely worried about winter, and homeless people freezing. He said homelessness was a big problem, and there definitely wasn't enough accommodation.

I think there are some areas you wouldn't be allowed to sleep out, like Point Grey, the British Properties. Most malls have "no loitering" signs. I saw a man sleeping on the sidewalk on Hastings. Police poked him, made him move on.

The Bag Lady is back on Main for the winter. She seems to travel west in summer. She was sleeping again at the store that has all the beds and mattresses in the window. It's well lit. She was sleeping under a pile of her possessions, all wrapped securely in garbage bags.

In the doorway
of the Mattress Store
bedded down
on your garbage
bags filled with
your secrets
that no one dare touch
You challenge
another winter

November

The police, in full armed riot gear, moved in and arrested the squatters on Frances Street. They tore down part of the houses with bulldozers. The police told the media that the squatters were armed and had a huge cache of weapons. The only arms visible were those of the police.

A large sign appeared on one of the houses: "VPD Rules."

Community people are asking for an enquiry: why was so much force used? Could it not have been done differently? The bottom line is that now those houses are gone to a developer, and nothing has been done to solve the problem of reasonable rent. Even though there was no demolition permit, the houses are now coming down because the police declared it was a dangerous situation, and the bulldozing had made them unstable.

The squatters' message seemed to get lost in the media, who played up the possibility of their being armed. Yes, there had been changes with some people at the squat, but the issue of gentrification and homelessness hadn't changed. Should homeless people stay out in the cold and the rain, should they sleep under viaducts and bridges, when good housing sits vacant waiting for speculators to manipulate the market?

Some Facts on Housing from the Civic Election Campaign

In 1989, Vancouver approved demolition of 588 rental units. In addition, 735 rental units were emptied out by people who were applying for demolition permits.

To date (October 1990), nine permits for family (also known as in-law) suites have been applied for. Sixty-four permits for permanent (also known as secondary) suites have been applied for. There are three hundred and five outstanding applications to phase out suites. The total number of secondary and in-law suites in the city is estimated at 26,000. The total cost to date of the program is estimated at $1,261,872 or $17,286 per legalized unit.

from TRAC

The one-year cost for operating an anti-submarine-warfare cruiser is $59,400,000.

This amount is equivalent to what it would cost to house

three-quarters of the homeless families in London, England for one year.

The 1987 global military expenditure was $1.8 million a minute.

from World Military Social Expenditures 1987-88

All 17,000 senior citizens, disabled persons and low-income families waiting for social housing in the Lower Mainland could be accommodated for the cost of just 36 hours of war.

Vancouver Sun, *February 4, 1991*

How can we find so much money for war but so very little to solve social problems and homelessness? War creates refugees, homeless people, orphaned children... thousands more homeless people when already in the world we have 100,000,000 people (according to UNICEF) who have no shelter whatsoever.

Donald Gutstein has a book out called *The New Landlords*. This book helped me to understand the real estate marketplace from the other side, the side where people have money. The governments have been encouraging off-shore investors to buy our homes, our communities, for their own financial interests. Politicians can change zoning and bylaws, take farmland out of the agricultural land reserve, and now our lives are held in the hands of others, real estate speculators, developers.

It was good to read his research. It confirmed my gut feeling about the reasons for homelessness and the housing crunch. One end of the spectrum is off-shore realtors taking over cities. The other end of the spectrum is workers and the poor losing their homes and communities. Homelessness is not accidental.

November 30, it's cold, wet, windy. My daughter asked me to stay in the car with the baby while she went to the bank machine on Main. I was sitting, looking out the car window. The parking lot was empty as it was early morning.

Then I saw Pierre. He was really dirty, terribly thin, his pants had holes in the back from sitting on them. He had his old black jacket on his skinny shoulders, and he carried a back pack. I saw him open the dumpster, eat something from it, then go to another dumpster and eat something from that one, too.

My impulse was to give him money for food, but I couldn't leave the baby. And would he know what to do with money, anyway? He is obviously mentally sick. He needs help, but has to be "well enough" to know that he needs help. Pierre was a baby once, he had a mother, father—what happened to him?

Bag Lady of Main
we crossed paths
you pushing your cart
overflowing with your
possessions
Hello said I
and you responded
with a beautiful
smile
Could this be
the beginning
of a wonderful
friendship

December

I saw Liz again at a friend's house. She hasn't got her children back. She visits them in their foster home. She looked pale, depressed. Another mother was there with her new baby. As everyone cooed over the baby, Liz sat on the floor in the corner. I was aware of her discomfort.

Liz and I shared a lift home. She said she was going to programs, looking for housing, just trying to hold it all together.

Christmas is coming—a horrendous, painful, body-wrenching time for people like Liz. To be homeless at Christmas and hear constant commercial Christmas jingles from November on, that jog the brain, that plays the tape, that tells you "There's something wrong with you when you have no home, no tree, no gifts."

I called Betty McPhee, the director of Crabtree Corners, and asked her how the situation was, had it improved, how were they coping? Betty said, "It's awful, just awful. Worse, much worse. I can't think of anything else to say except it's just awful. There is no other way I can describe it."

I checked around the community and the general consensus is that the situation is worse.

Mugs Sigurgeirson, Carnegie Association

There are many wonderful people living in the downtown eastside in private homes, social housing, co-ops, apartments, hotel rooms, etc. There are families, children, singles, seniors—healthy, community-minded people, the very finest people you would want to have as neighbours. Everybody, everything isn't

Percentage of Clients with Reported Shelter Costs Exceeding Shelter Allowance by Region (January, 1989)

	Van. Richmd Delta %	N. Van. Howe Sd %	Fraser North %	Fraser South %	Oknagn Kootenay %	Central Interior %	Prince George %	North %	North Island Cariboo %	South Island %
Single men	38.2	26.7	47.7	50.9	32.2	33.7	40.8	34.7	37.7	45.0
Single women	45.7	39.3	56.5	58.3	44.5	46.6	49.2	45.0	49.3	55.1
Couples	53.4	39.6	55.8	57.8	37.9	29.9	26.1	21.7	37.0	51.1
Two parents with										
one child	48.5	42.9	49.4	58.2	24.1	24.8	18.2	14.5	32.3	47.2
two children	41.6	27.1	59.7	60.5	26.3	22.7	23.3	17.9	30.0	40.1
three children	39.2	29.1	58.8	49.7	32.8	17.0	14.6	17.1	27.4	48.8
four children	43.8	37.8	58.9	65.7	27.4	31.2	15.7	30.9	37.0	53.3
One parent with										
one child	46.2	44.5	53.1	56.0	31.5	31.7	28.4	25.9	42.7	49.8
two children	45.2	44.0	58.1	62.3	34.3	29.9	26.5	19.4	37.1	50.7
three children	49.3	42.8	61.2	61.6	29.4	25.5	24.5	15.6	35.3	47.9
four children	52.2	43.6	67.9	68.6	24.6	24.1	16.4	14.5	34.8	53.2

Source: Data provided by Ministry of Social Services and Housing (February, 1990). Reprinted from *Closing the Gap*, by Michael Goldberg, published by the Social Planning and Research Council of British Columbia (SPARC), April 1990.

Percentage of Income Assistance Recipients Reporting Shelter Costs Greater Than GAIN Shelter Allowance by Family Type and Size (N = 81,215)

Family type and size	No. of cases	Max. GAIN allwnce	% over allwnce Jan. '90	% over allwnce Jan. '89	% over allwnce Jan. '88
Single Men	27,223	$275	37.4	36.4	28.9
Single Women	14,840	$275	48.8	49.9	39.6
Couple	2,120	$446	42.4	44.7	32.7
2 parents with					
one child	1,952	$514	38.0	39.1	30.0
two children	2,084	$560	37.1	40.7	30.9
three children	1,190	$600	33.8	37.5	29.3
four children	218	*	*	*	*
One parent with					
one child	15,510	$446	43.9	46.5	33.3
two children	10,633	$514	43.8	45.8	33.9
three children	3,811	$560	41.8	46.0	34.1
four children	914	$600	42.5	40.3	35.8
more than four	244	*	*	*	*

* Given the small numbers, disaggregated analysis of shelter cost is not presented for families with more than four children.
Source: Data provided by Ministry of Social Services and Housing (February, 1990). Reprinted from *Closing the Gap*.

Skid Road, even though there are more bars here than anywhere else in Vancouver.

One of these people is Mugs Sigurgeirson, president of the Carnegie Association. Mugs has been one of the movers and groovers in the Strathcona Community Gardens, a garden of allotment plots where community people grow their veggies. It has an acre of community herb gardens, an orchard, and a social area. In the middle is an acre they call natural marsh and wild land. All this is right in the heart of the downtown eastside.

Homeless people have lived in the marshland, and still do. Mugs told me about two women that lived there. One turned tricks in the compost heap, leaving used condoms around. The other woman did glue. She was mentally sick and would hide in the blackberry bush, in a hole small enough for a rabbit. Garden-

Adequacy of Maximum Shelter Allowance in Meeting Shelter Costs Using MSSH Definition of Affordable Housing

(Basic rent set at 25th percentile)

	Basic Rent $	Utilities $	Telephone $	Total Shelter $	Current Ceiling $	Shortfall $	Shortfall %
Single male (bachelor)	385	13.72	15.65	414.37	275	139.37	51
Single parent son - 5 (two bedroom)	565	16.90	15.65	597.55	446	151.55	34
Couple (one-bedroom)	450	14.26	15.65	479.91	446	33.91	8
Single parent Son - 16 Daughter - 14 (three-bedroom)	680	16.90	15.65	712.55	514	198.55	39
Couple Daughter - 5 Infant - 6 months (three-bedroom)	680	16.90	15.65	712.55	560	152.55	27

Reprinted from *Closing the Gap*.

ers would hear her singing "Stormy Weather" and other old songs.

One Saturday Mugs and the gardening group had a clean-up of the wild lands. They do it yearly. They collected a deep freeze, a cigarette machine, a couch, mattress, seven tires, parts of car motors, tools, buckets, junk, blankets, used condoms. We both wondered what kind of john would want to have his trick in the compost heap.

Next to the allotment is Strathcona Park. Once there was a hobo camp there. It was well organized. About 15 men had a huge tarp thrown over a tree, and they cooked over an open fire. They survived.

Along the back of the park there is a neglected industrial strip. Old buses, broken down cars, and vans line the street. Homeless people live there. The park has toilets and hot water, so it's well used by the homeless. A big problem is rats and garbage. Mugs knew a woman named Pattie who lived on that strip in an old vehicle for a year. She kept the street clean, but there's lots of garbage there now.

Proportion of Units Available
(in Greater Vancouver)
Rents Near Maximum GAIN Shelter Allowance

Type of Unit	Number of People	Maximum GAIN Shelter Allowance $	CMHC Rent Range $	Oct. 1989 %	Oct. 1988 %	Oct. 1987 %
Bachelor	1 person	275	0-299	2.0	2.5	3.8
1 bedroom	1 person	275	0-299	0.2	0.1	0.1
	2 people	446	0-459	23.9	25.2	42.8
2 bedroom	2 people	446	0-459	1.8	0.9	3.2
	3 people	514	0-539	11.0	16.0	30.5
3 bedroom	3 people	514	0-539	1.5	2.8	8.3
	4 people	560	0-579	7.0	7.3	19.9
	5 people	600	0-619	11.4	17.0	32.2
	6 people	619	0-619	11.4	25.2	48.8

Note: Maximum shelter allowances and CMHC rent ranges were lower in 1988 and 1987.

Source: Canada Mortgage and Housing Corporation (October, 1989); reprinted from *Closing the Gap*.

Many of the people living in this area are junk collecters, scavengers. I call them recyclers. They collect tons of junk and stash it, creating another garbage problem when they abandon it.

Strathcona parents are seriously concerned. Children are scared when they come to school and see homeless people sleeping in the doorways. A janitor is hired to pick up the needles and condoms that are scattered over the school yard. It's done early in the morning to make the yard safe for the kids.

Mugs told me that the redevelopment of downtown Granville for middle-class singles will see the destruction and demise of 300 low-rental rooms. Her suggested solutions are: more shelters, more temporary shelters. There's a desperate need for drug and alcohol counselling right in the downtown eastside for people who live there. We need more real services. We need more housing for the mentally sick. If it wasn't for the housing shortage, our shelters wouldn't be filled.

We know how to do it, there's just no money.

Homelessness and the Housing Crisis
by Leslie Timmins, YWCA Vancouver Housing Registry

A few years ago when Toronto was experiencing as bad a housing crisis as we are now in Vancouver, a friend of mine was going to school there and sharing an apartment with a young man who was having a hard time emotionally. In January, the house their suite was in was sold on the hot housing market, and they couldn't find another place to live. My friend moved in with her mother in the suburbs; the young man, whose family wasn't supportive, moved into his car, and a short while later committed suicide.

Lack of affordable housing is one of the causes of homelessness, which in turn contributes to other tragedies. Fortunately, most of the homeless people I see in my job at the YWCA's Vancouver Housing Registry seem to be coping with their situation, which isn't to say that it's easy. Shirley, who's fifty, has been living in an abandoned building for three months because her welfare cheque won't cover the cost of a place where she can have her own bathroom. She's angry and wants to sue the government. But two other women living in a station wagon, I do worry about.

A hotel room in the Silver Lodge before it was closed down

I noticed their car outside my office because a cat was sitting on the headrest in the front seat, cleaning his paws, and another was sleeping in the back on a pile of suitcases. These women have been travelling around, one of them older and in poor health, trying to find a place they can afford which will also let them keep their pets. In this housing crisis, that's almost an impossible dream.

Most of the one thousand or so people who use the Housing Registry every month do have a roof over their heads, but it's not necessarily their own roof. If you ask these people, they too would say they're homeless. They include single mothers living in transition houses for months because they can't go back to their violent husbands and they can't find an affordable suite which will accept their kids. Other people, like Wendy and her children, have crowded, temporarily, into a friend's house. Even though she has a job, Wendy says she's got two strikes against her: she's native and she's a single mom. At the Registry we've seen so many cases of discrimination against families like this that the YWCA formally asked for amendments to the B.C. Human Rights Code to protect children and the poor in housing.

If home is a place where we feel *at home*, at ease, safe, where our kids are welcome, then we could broaden the definition of homelessness even more. Many poor people in Vancouver are living in what is at best third-rate housing—run-down, damp, or in the case of single moms again, over-crowded. These people may not be living in the streets, but they're not in homes either.

It's obvious that the common thread in homelessness is poverty. Some of the solutions then may be: welfare rates which correspond to the real housing situation; more (truly affordable) rental housing; more social housing; measures to hold onto the rental stock that's left in Vancouver; and an effective rent review system.

A home gives us a sense of control over our lives. Homelessness takes it away. The plight of the young man in Toronto, and all homeless people, shows us plainly that housing is a vital human need which cannot be left to "market forces"; it must instead be raised to one of our governments' and our communities' highest priorities.

The Children

Although nation-wide data are not available, the number of homeless youth in Canada is shocking. Existing services simply cannot accommodate the tens of thousands of young people who are drifting in cities and urban centres. Unable to stay at home because of family problems, they often cannot find suitable housing, and when they do, too often cannot afford it.
    Report of the Special Committee on Youth, 1986, p.12; quoted in Street Youth and AIDS

There are as many as 150,000 homeless street kids in Canadian cities. They come from all walks of life. They don't fit the stereotype 'street kid'.
    Covenant House Brochure, 1988, p. 5; quoted in Street Youth and AIDS

Pablo, of DEYAS, said that one problem is that "prostitution offers a lot more money than what we can offer as a society. [Kids] live with, crash with families that don't take care of them. They go to visit their mother's friend, and mother's friend is an alcoholic, so they come late at night when everybody is asleep so they don't have to deal with the level of violence and alcoholism of the house. Some of them have to sell their bodies to be able to get a place to sleep. I know males out there that just come down, take one of these kids, and then invite them for a joint of marijuana or coke—just to convince them that they should spend the night with them. Obviously more girls—but boys too. There's a boys town up on Granville—runaways. People use these kids and when they're finished with them, they kick them out. People pimp them, beat them, use them to carry drugs. So when the police stop them, they are clean, but the kid, the one beside him, is the one carrying the drugs."

A runaway is a child who is most often thrown from his home or asked to leave his home by a very angry, a very depressed, a very drunk [or] a very high on drugs parent who simply cannot cope with [his or her] own problem, and that these kids are forced out. It is very rare that these kids want to run. Most children want to go home. They are not carefree children.
    M.D. Janus A. McCormack, A.W. Burgess and C. Hartman, 1987, p. 12; *quoted in* Street Youth and AIDS

Karen O'Shannacery, Lookout: "Kids are in a double bind because if they present themselves or ask for any kind of assistance from any group funded by the government, they have to be turned over to the government, and of course then they're sent back home to whatever it is they are running away from. We know there's kids out there, and occasionally, very very rarely, we'll have a child come in and ask us for assistance. But we're caught in the bind—we have to call Emergency Services and say to a social worker, we've got an underage child here, and of course the kids don't want that, so they don't come here."

Most of the youth described their peer support system on the street as fundamental to their basic existence. Isolation while on the street is fraught with risks...Street friends are like family, depended upon for social interaction, nurturance, love and protection.
    from Street Youth and AIDS.

Karen Gallagher, YWCA: "I think there are more kids out there than we are aware of, but how we collect those statistics...I really don't know. They feel very disenfranchised from society in general, so why should they co-operate with us to get that information? This group needs to feel safe before they can give us any information.

"I would bet my paycheque that the kids that are out on the street, are on the street because it's unsafe for them to be at home, or unsuitable for them to be in foster placement. The system has

Number of street youth by type and gender

Type	Male	Female	Total
Homeless	138	131	269
Youthful offender	91	21	112
Unemployed	70	82	152
Prostitute	42	57	99
Drug abuser	50	30	80
Total	**391**	**321**	**712**

Reprinted from *Street Youth and AIDS*, by Joyce L. Radford, Alan J.C. King, and Wendy K. Warren, Queen's University, 1989.

broken down and basically they're the victims of systemic breakdown.

"I think there needs to be a holistic coming together of all the people who work with teens that are homeless, including the teenagers themselves, to look at solutions for their own needs."

Vancouver Social Planning Department

I went to City Hall to interview Rita Chudnovsky, Rick Gates, and Jeff Brooks of the Social Planning Department. Rita is the child advocate for the city of Vancouver.

"The job of child advocate is really broadly defined as making Vancouver a better place for kids, and to work with community groups and levels of government to do that. I don't have any power, beyond the power to recommend to city council and to lobby senior levels of government, and to try to work with community organizations as they request, to help them get the resources to find solutions to the problems they're facing. I don't have a budget I control, don't have a staff to control. It's the power to influence, and the power to sit down and try to help people work out solutions.

"A large part of the work I'm involved in is trying to look at what can and should we be doing, when kids are younger and families are trying to deal with young children, that will break some of the cycles that lead to the situation where kids are on the street.

"Crabtree Corner recently got a native alcohol and drug counsellor to deal with the increasing number of fetal alcohol syndrome kids. One of the real problems is a lot of the kids on the street experience physical and sexual abuse at home, and the street's a better alternative. We have a huge gap in lack of treatment. When physical or sexual abuse is identified—if it is—and it is reported, then there is *some* intervention of the criminal justice system, maybe. But we offer very little help to those kids. So there's been an inter-ministerial proposal—some money has been allocated and I'm waiting to see how it's to be spent—to set up a co-ordinated physical and sexual abuse treatment program that would bring together some of the services now in the community and would add to it, so that families who have gone through that could get some early help to deal with it so the cycles don't continue.

"When you talk about homeless kids and kids on the street, there's a whole series of issues about why they got there and how they got there. I don't think my viewpoint on homelessness is going to be any different than yours. There's homeless families with kids because there's not enough affordable, secure housing.

Street youth by gender and age

Male / Female

% of respondents

Age	15		16		17		18		19		20	
Male	8		21		29		23		17		3	
Female		13		27		25		17		14		3

Source: *Street Youth and Aids.*

It's like when people ask me why there's poverty, I say it's because families don't have enough income!

"On top of the lack of affordable housing in general, there is a lot of discrimination against families with kids, there's a lot of discrimination against single mothers on welfare, and there's racism. Not only does that go on in the community, it's basically legally allowed. The provincial government recently amended the Residential Tenancy Act and says it will end discrimination. I don't buy that. It's very very ineffective. I've been working for a change to the Human Rights Act to at least give it a legal basis, but even if we eliminate the right to discriminate legally, we don't disagree that we need to be finding ways to provide affordable, secure, adequate, safe housing.

"I think there's some great things I've seen and heard about that can be done to develop housing for families, that helps to support families and allows single moms or isolated women to

Street youth sample by city

City	%
Toronto	20
Montreal	18
Vancouver	14
Winnipeg	10
Edmonton	9
Halifax	8
Ottawa	8
St. John's	5
Saskatoon	5
Kenora	3

Source: *Street Youth and Aids.*

come together and share some of the cooking. DERA's done some of that.

"More needs to be done. There are a growing number of kids in the city that live in families that live in poverty, and the way to address that is to raise the minimum wage, to raise welfare rates, to create training programs so women can get decent jobs, to have affordable childcare, and not to bring in policies, like the GST and cuts to UI, that put families further into poverty.

"I hear a lot from parents about certain kinds of programs not being there for kids. I hear a lot from people in contact, through community organizations, with kids who they see have some needs. Everything from housing to food to mental health services to family support. And there's a real level of frustration because, even though daycare workers and school teachers can see at an early age that help right then and there could make a difference, the help isn't there till we get to a crisis situation. I hear a lot of that frustration—'If only we could give some support to this family now in a difficult period.'

"One of the things the city is doing is purchasing portables to lease to non-profit groups for $1 a year, for childcare programs. The first group trying to get it off the ground is at Strathcona School, where the parents have been on a three-year campaign because of the number of kids on their own after school in not a safe environment. They're concerned about the kind of connections being made with very young kids. There's about $100,000 going into a portable to provide before and after school care for kids from 5 to 12. But at that very front-line level, if we don't start meeting those kids' needs, they're going to be the next kids [on the street].

"I don't think services are the only solution, but services are sure a part of it. I hear a lot about lack of services—lack of mental health services, safe recreational programs.

"I certainly have heard there's an increased number of families with young kids in the downtown eastside. It also goes without saying that this is not an appropriate place for families to be raising children. I want to sit down with community organizations; we need to start thinking about that community as a place with small children, because it's only recently that people have started to think about or talk about the fact that there are more and more kids in the downtown eastside, and clearly that's not a place where kids should go.

"People talk a lot about the problem of a lack of resources in the community for kids who can't live at home, for whatever reason. There are not sufficient group homes and foster homes in the area, so kids are often put in foster homes or group homes in Coquitlam and Delta, and of course they run away because those kids are ripped out of their neighbourhoods. How can we start to build those community residences, and how can we build that safe housing? I think some of the really good examples of good housing are Entre Nous Femmes, non-profit housing society for single moms. I think they're great. They're not the only ones, but they're one of the models."

Social Planning has been working with the ministry and other groups. Rick Gates, of the street kids committee, and Jeff Brooks, the clinic administrator of the Vancouver Health Department, would like to see a "safe house." That would be a shelter from which children couldn't be apprehended, but where they could have perhaps a few days "time out" to think things through. The details are not yet finalized. Jeff Brooks told me about this project.

"The first part of it was to identify where, potentially, the kids thought would be a good place, and we looked at the Granville area, and identified an area in the city. The second part is for MSSH to identify the money for operating funds, so if the city is willing to give the land for $1 a year or whatever, we need the operating funds.

"The police have been involved, MSSH, the street kids themselves have made these recommendations, and the non-profit services. If we can get one going, hopefully we can get two going, maybe one in the downtown eastside.

"That's one phase. The second part is an alcohol and drug detox for all these street kids.

"Finally, after I don't know how many reports, we have a proposal to look for joint funding for next year. This is a priority for Vancouver."

The people in Social Planning were genuinely concerned. One asked me "Why is it that, even when we move these kids out of the downtown, they run back?" Well, as the report *Street Kids and AIDS* says, the people of the street are the only family some of these kids know. Rita said, "I think we have to find ways to bring those kids out of no-person-land. I think we have to find ways to provide those kids with economic support, but not *just* economic support—medical coverage, and an in to the services, health and education, that they're hesitant to go for. Maybe today, age 19 [as the age of 'adulthood'] is not realistic; lots of people are on their own well before 19, and are working, or not working, or are on welfare or raising a family.

"As well as looking at that whole age question, there's going to be individual cases where there's going to have to be flexibility. Some people should be getting the kind of support that we say should go to youth, even after the legal age, and other people need to be given the support that goes with adult responsibility below the age."

Hotel kids

The July 6 headline in the *Province* said: "Hotel kids plight—ministry faces shortage of foster and group homes."

One hotel manager said his hotel wasn't good for kids. A door was smashed during a fight outside a room where four children —aged 8, 4, 2, and 1—were sleeping.

A social worker with ten years' experience said the ministry was subjecting kids "to more emotional trauma by dumping them in sleazy fleabag hotels with a homemaker. We would probably step in and apprehend children from the situation in which our own ministry is placing kids."

Since April, according to the *Province*, the ministry had lodged 30 children in Vancouver hotels with homemakers. Children come from situations of sexual and physical abuse, and find themselves apprehended, living in hotel rooms (placed there by the ministry). They are then exposed to drugs, violence, prostitution, and all the other negative aspects of street life.

When these homeless children are moved from room to room, they get even more messed up. Will they be the next decade of homeless people? By abusing abused children, we set the scene for them to become disfunctional adults. We will then blame them, the victims, when they don't cope in the society we created for them. Cutbacks in social services, privatization of group homes, giving services over to profitmaking—these children are the victims of the marketplace philosophy.

Andrea

Andrea is in her late teens. I talked with her in the Ovaltine Cafe on Hastings. She came to Vancouver when she ran away from home. Her father had been having sex with her since she was 10. She hated him, so took off and hitchhiked here. Sometimes she had to give sex for a meal or for a ride. People who she asked to help her just wanted to send her back to her father. She thought that no one believed her. Her mother didn't.

"I survived. I've got a job and a boyfriend now. It's not too bad except when he drinks he gets real mad and I get scared of him. He's hit me a few times...It could be worse...At least I'm not hooking. When I came here and I had no place to sleep I couldn't go for help because they would have sent me back. So I'd pick up a man if he had a place. Then I'd go home with him. It was safer than being on the streets. Of course I'd have to let them do what they wanted to my body. That's the price of a place to stay isn't it? One guy brought his friends back to the room and they took turns using my body...There was nothing I could do...It was real nasty.

"It's better now though. I'm 19 and there's no fucking way they can send me back. I work as a waitress down the street. Sometimes I get pissed just to forget. Sometimes I do drugs but not much."

"Homelessness is being scared to go home...Homelessness is having to have sex for a place to sleep...Homelessness is no one caring about you, like not belonging anywhere...I think I'm pregnant. I know my baby would love me....But my boyfriend's not too happy about it."

Jo

We met in a coffee shop on Commercial Drive. She was 15, a small fragile girl with a shy smile and huge grey eyes. A friend introduced me to her. Her name was Jo. She told me her mother had kicked her out when she was 13. Her mother had paid 100 dollars a month for her to stay with a friend of the mother's, but it hadn't lasted for long. She wouldn't stay in a group home, so she was living on the street. A friend took her to stay with a woman who let her stay at the house for free, but she had to do the housework, the laundry, take care of the three young children. The woman was an alcoholic. There was a lot of partying in the house. Jo said she didn't get any money for the work, just room and board. She said she was really scared for the children. They were not being very well looked after. A short time later the woman threw her out. I don't know where Jo went. I asked her once about school. She hadn't been since she was 12. She said, "I just can't hack school or group homes, and my mother doesn't want me."

Carol

The Women's Centre was busy. Melanie had made baked beans and another volunteer had cooked some bannock. It was great. It was miserable weather, the rain was pouring down, so the food was really enjoyed.

Carol came over as I was talking to Melanie about homelessness. She told me she was staying in a hotel on Hastings with her two teenage daughters because rents were so high. She said she couldn't get rooms side by side, so the girls were down the hall and round the corner from her. There wasn't a washroom in their room; they had to use a communal one down the hall. Carol had been sharing a house with someone. They left, and she couldn't afford to pay all the rent. Carol said she hoped to stay only a month at this hotel, but it was hard to find affordable rentals.

She said because she is a woman of colour, and because she has teenagers, it was really difficult to find a place. Carol had been on the waiting list for three years for B.C. Housing. She called them but they had no record of her application. When she had changed addresses, she hadn't understood that she had to mail cards to them with address changes, so that they could keep in touch. They said they would send her a new application. She asked, "Does this mean I have to start all over again?"

In the meantime, there are no cooking facilities in her room, so she and her daughters eat at the 44, the Women's Centre, and at restaurants when they have the money. Carol works part time as a waitress, but her health isn't great. She said she had never ever put her kids in care, in spite of lots of problems. She had never given up her kids and said she never would.

THE CHILDREN

Carol's definition of homelessness is anyone without a home —a hotel room isn't a home.

Anna, Carol's daughter, was sitting nearby, huddled up on the couch, a beautiful, gentle-looking girl with long black hair and big soft brown eyes. I asked her if I could talk to her about homelessness. She was very shy.

"Homeless is having no food...and no furniture...A home should have food and furniture.

"When I come home from school I just go to my room and listen to my radio. It's so boring, nothing to do but sit in the room. No food, just water to drink. There's so many cockroaches. I don't let anyone in school know where I live...We eat at the 44...I'm not in school today, I just couldn't make it."

Carol said Anna had missed a lot of school.

To look at Anna you would see a clean, neatly dressed, beautiful young girl who could be from Point Grey. She wouldn't be a homeless statistic, she wouldn't be visibly homeless.

I wanted to hug her. I wanted to make everything okay for her. I wanted her to finish school. She's in grade 10. I wanted her to have a fair chance. I know what she is up against.

This is another story that doesn't have an ending.

I never met the younger teenager. One thing though, the most important thing, there was obviously love there; Carol loved her kids.

John Turvey, DEYAS: "Something social workers are being forced to do more and more frequently is to place people in hotel rooms, and not just adult individuals. We're talking about whole families, and usually single parent families, usually with a mother. You can see them some mornings in front of the Patricia Hotel and places like that, trying to get their kids out of the area before the whole day kicks into gear. Like, this is the most dangerous strip in western Canada! If not in Canada. So here we've got it being used as some sort of crisis facility. So there's more and more of that kind of use of hotel rooms. What it indicates is that there hasn't been a development of the resources."

Karen Howe, First United Church: "It's becoming more and more common for families to be facing housing crises. Just this morning, for example, I had a couple with a 9-year-old girl who were evicted from their house because they didn't pay the rent. They had given their rent money to a brother who had left town with it. They had been evicted without appropriate notice. They didn't have any way of fighting back. They had lost their personal possessions that had taken them four years to accumulate. They are now living in a hotel room. The child had two toys. They are trying to feed her, clothe her, trying to make her feel she is in a stable environment. They slept out on the street as a family last Monday. They will have to stay in the hotel till the end of the month, or until they can get an apartment.

"The ministry creates a situation where it's unstable for the kids, like placing families in hotels. Then they apprehend the kids."

No Kids Ban Worsens Lot of Vancouver's One-Parent Families

by Noreen Shanahan

Vancouver watches as women are forced to pack up their children, vacate their homes, and look for another place to live. In their search, however, they often find landlords standing on the other side of an "Adult Only" sign, barring their entrance.

The city's current housing crisis translates into greater discrimination against women and children. Considered undesirable tenants, families increasingly have no other option than to cram into a hotel room, most often in Vancouver's downtown eastside.

"Women tell us they're forced into hotels, forced into raising kids in one stinking little room," says Karen Gallagher of the Vancouver Housing Registry.

"It's a landlord's market these days, and they get to 'skim the cream' as far as who they'll rent to. With scores of people on waiting lists, tenants have to jump through hoops just to be considered."

And women trailing kids behind them don't often make it through these hoops.

Margo MacGuire lives in a hotel with her two teenage children. Since arriving from Toronto a year ago, she has already watched one east end home be demolished and another burn to the ground due to bad wiring. She's now searching for a third.

"Last week I phoned 49 places from the paper, and was allowed to see only seven of them. They never say it's rented until after I say I have kids. If my kids were smaller I'd hide them, and wouldn't say anything till after we move in and then watch them try to kick us out."

The Ministry of Social Services and Housing (MSSH) first tried to book them into a women's shelter, she said, but shelter waiting lists closed off this option. Instead, MacGuire considers herself privileged to be living outside the downtown eastside (although she uses the area's services).

Another woman frequently seen at the Downtown Eastside Women's Centre clutching the day's "suites to rent" ads is Tracy (not her real name), the mother of four girls aged 9, 10, 11, and 12.

Tracy moved her family into the area early last summer, after being forced out of their decrepit Mount Pleasant suite, where the landlord continually refused to do necessary repairs.

In her search for a new home, she most commonly hears landlords say "you have too many children."

"I know other women with kids who are waiting five months to find a home, living in shelters or hotels or with relatives; sharing anything with a roof over their heads. You have no choice when you have children, as long as it's a roof."

According to Kim Nightingale, co-ordinator of the Downtown Eastside Women's Centre, women are moving into the area at a disturbing rate.

"We get calls from transition houses, DERA (Downtown Eastside Residents Association), St. James, MSSH, all saying 'we have women with kids who can't find housing' and we say 'sure, send them all down.' (The Women's Centre doesn't house these families, but welcomes them into the area.)

"And these single mothers aren't stupid; they know this is a lousy area to raise kids, and they wouldn't do it if they had any other choice."

The women's and children's physical safety is a particular concern in the community. According to Betty McPhee at Crabtree Corner Daycare, assaults on women in the area are increasing at an alarming rate. "Minor assaults aren't reported, but a growing number of aggravated assaults—when ambulances are called—are being documented."

Hotel security is frighteningly faulty, she said, leaving the family vulnerable to attack. Two women were recently raped in their rooms.

"Hotel room doors can be opened so easily, which also leaves the children at risk," says McPhee. "What often happens is on [welfare] cheque day someone gets into the room, takes a look around to see if anything new was bought, and then takes all the family's possessions.

"This leaves the family homeless and on the street. We try to get them into transition shelters, but they're already overbooked."

Many believe raising children in a hotel is a last option, but according to Nightingale, hotels are also turning single mothers away, in effect implementing their own "adult only" restriction.

According to John Shayler of the Tenants Rights Coalition, a recent trend by management in cheaper hotels is to raise the rent. This not only deters the most economically desperate from living there, but it also effectively wipes out any legal tenant protections.

"Recent amendments to the Residential Tenancy Act cover hotel residents, providing they're 'permanent' [have no other address] and don't pay over $450 per month."

Nightingale says one downtown eastside hotel recently shot its monthly rate up from $450 to $700.

These restrictions leave women with even fewer housing choices, and dreams of "security" become little more than fantasy.

Discrimination in rental housing is, unfortunately, as old as rental housing itself. Nor is it the first time Vancouver has been confronted with homelessness. The contemporary twist, however—leaving more families homeless—is compounded by many factors.

Secondary suite closures: Single mothers are traditionally given rental market dregs, partly because it's all they can afford, but also because the old maxim "children are to be seen and not heard" applies in housing. Many landlords also require they be pretty well hidden away—in basements, or above garages—so other tenants aren't "bothered" by them.

Vancouver's present vacancy rate of 0.4 percent translates into 282 suites available at any one time.

Shortly after this statistic was released by the Canadian Mortgage and Housing Corporation (CMHC), Vancouver city council threatened closure of 280 secondary suites, housing a large number of single mothers on welfare. A total of 26,000 secondary suites are threatened.

Demolitions: Since January, over a thousand people in Vancouver have lost their homes to the wrecking ball—most of them women, many of them with children.

Roneen Marcoux, a researcher hired by the city who compiled this data, was shocked at the extent of affordable housing being destroyed and the effect it was having on women she interviewed.

"Single women with children were turned away time and time again," says Marcoux. "One woman tried to find a place for herself, her teenaged daughter and her mother but the landlords would reject her, saying 'and what about your husband?'

"They equate single parent families with total poverty; there was a great deal of economic discrimination happening."

Decline of rental subsidies: Subsidized social housing units have declined to the lowest levels in this decade, falling from 1,405 in 1985 to 425 in 1988, according to David Hulchanski at the Centre for Human Settlements.

Furthermore, B.C. Housing Management regulations deny subsidy to women under 45 years. Gail Meredith, director at the downtown eastside's Mavis McMullen House, said their building —containing 34 units—fought to convince B.C. Housing to include younger women in their mandate. "We managed to change it to age 35, arguing that living in the area ages women."

Renovations, condo-style: With the mighty swipe of the bulldozer, affordable "homes" are being replaced by luxury "condos." Throughout the city, women and children are being evicted to make way for "extensive renovations."

One landlord in a west end building containing 86 units, and between 70 and 100 children, has sent almost everyone an eviction notice.

In two months, renovations begin and predictions are that within a year, management will demand out-of-reach rents and children will not be allowed to live there.

The west end is already out of reach for most parents. In fact, this building is one of few remaining where children are allowed.

After a determined search, Sarah Marchant and her husband

gave up on the west end. Although they fit the bill of "family" which many landlords require, there simply weren't any buildings which allow children.

"We must have looked at 50 places when finally a woman let us in and showed us around some really nice suites," says Marchant. "Then she asked us, 'Is this your child?' I said yes, and she said 'We don't take kids here.'

"It was almost as though she couldn't believe we had the nerve to come and look at the place, with a kid."

It's illegal to evict a woman simply because she's a mother. Instead, landlords are "cleaning up their tenancies" by harassing women out. And although the Residential Tenancy Act protects people from harassment, this protection is rarely enforced.

Karen Fletcher has lived with her four children, for the past seven years, in a two bedroom basement suite. A couple of months ago, she called the landlord in to repair the toilet. In September, he finally got the plumbing bill.

"He said that either I pay half the bill ($250) or he'll raise my rent $200 a month," says Fletcher.

This is clear harassment, she says, intended to get her out. Her children are the only ones left renting, not only in the building, but on that entire Mount Pleasant block.

Age discrimination allowed: Just as a developer's dream of "adult only" buildings translates into discrimination against women and children, so too does this particular discrimination translate into age preference.

Under the B.C. Human Rights Act, age discrimination in tenancies is allowed, although it is specifically prohibited in all other sections of the Act.

Section 5 (b) reads: "No person shall discriminate... because of the race, colour, ancestry, place of origin, religion, marital status, physical or mental disability or sex of that person or class of persons, or of any other person or class of persons."

"The reason for the exclusion in tenancies," says Suzi Kilgour of the Tenants Rights Coalition, "boils down to feudal property rights of man [sic]; that a man has the right to dictate what happens to his property... and the belief that people with children will ruin his property more than people without children."

However she says, this age discrimination contradicts protections in Section 15 of the Canadian Charter of Rights and Freedoms, which applies equally to children as members of Canadian society.

Legal steps necessary to end child discrimination in B.C. require a Charter challenge, says Carolyn McCool, a lawyer with Gastown Legal Services. And the legal argument would be made on the basis of "sex discrimination" as well as "age discrimination," since the impact of this form of housing discrimination is invariably on single, low-income women.

"We need to find a client, a woman, who's looking for a place to live and gets turned away at the door; who is facing actual discrimination," says McCool.

Why aren't women coming forward to fight this extremely crucial legal challenge?

To answer this question, one need only think back to when you were last threatened with eviction; when you last searched desperately for a home, a roof over your children's heads...

When confronted with so basic and essential a need, one has scant energy left to fight for anything more.

Once, and if, the legal battle is won, will it truly be able to protect women and their children when a landlord greets "more desirable" people standing in line waiting to view the suite?

In Ontario, where human rights legislation prohibits tenancy discrimination on the basis of "family status" and "receipt of public assistance [welfare]," landlords continue to operate with a free hand in a "free market."

Bruce Porter of Ontario's CERA (Centre for Equality Rights in Accommodation) says, out of 334 discrimination cases they dealt with last year, 40 percent were family status complaints.

They're presently faced with a legal challenge, where the owner of a condo turned a woman away because of the age of her child.

"Therefore adult only buildings argue discrimination isn't based on family status but it's based on age of occupant; they say 'We don't care if it's your child or not, we care about how old the kid is.'"

And so, for mothers from one end of the country to the other, the fight to find a secure roof for themselves and their children continues.

Copyright © 1989 by Noreen Shanahan. Reprinted with permission of the author.

'Adult Only Housing Discriminates Against Kids'

When Audrey Cope found out that she was pregnant, she also found herself without a home. The Adults Only policy in their apartment in Victoria forced Audrey and her husband to leave. They had to move all the way to Parksville to find a place that they could afford and where kids are accepted.

There is nothing in the B.C. Human Rights Act that protects people from this, even though the B.C. Human Rights Coalition lobbied the B.C. government to prohibit rental discrimination based on age and family status.

Audrey decided that something should be done about this so that other families don't have to go through the same harassment. Audrey decided to sue the provincial government.

Gwen Brodsky and Anita Braha, two lawyers from B.C. Public Interest Advocacy Center (BCPIAC), are representing Cope. They are arguing that the B.C. Human Rights Act violates the Charter of Rights and Freedoms because the Act fails to protect parents and kids from discrimination by landlords.

This is an important legal case because discrimination against children and families is so widespread and is still considered acceptable in B.C.. Throughout most of Europe, it is unheard of for families and children to be refused housing. Other provinces have done something to protect families' rights. Why hasn't B.C.? "The premier is very protective of the unborn, but where are children supposed to live?" asks Audrey Cope.

from FLAWline: B.C.'s Front Line Advocacy Workers' Newsletter, *May 15, 1990*

Since this case was begun, the B.C. provincial government has introduced Bill 51, an amendment to the Residential Tenancy Act that prohibits discrimination in rental housing on the basis of family status.

Housing advocates question the effectiveness of the proposed bill, however. In an article published in the Vancouver *Sun* on July 26, 1990, Laura Stannard of the Tenants Rights Coalition pointed out some of the problems with the bill.

Discrimination in housing has always been covered by the B.C. Human Rights Act, not the Residential Tenancy Act. "In effect," says Stannard, "the government is saying that family status discrimination is somehow different from other kinds of discrimination." It also means that the Human Rights Council may not have jurisdiction to rule on a form of discrimination that is not referred to in its act. And there are no discrimination cases heard by the Residential Tenancy Branch. Where will a family take its case if it has been refused housing because of children?

Bill 51 also allows exemptions that could cause problems. It makes it possible for a landlord "to refuse a designated handicapped suite to a disabled person with a child." It also allows cabinet to exclude any rental unit it wants.

If a landlord wants to evict tenants because there are too many people in the unit, he must give 24 months' notice, not the current one month, if the additional person is a child. This sounds good, but Stannard points out, "This means the government will protect a child for two years. Discrimination against babies would be against the law, but after two years the protection is inexplicably removed."

Stannard concludes, "Bill 51 does not give renters protection against exorbitant rent increases and it certainly does not stop developers from tearing down the last square feet of affordable rental housing. Bill 51 does not address security of tenure ... Make no mistake about it: Bill 51 will not make affordable rental housing any more accessible to families or to anyone else."

Solutions

Will the Socreds Sell Your Home?

by Pam Fleming

The Socreds have privatized everything from natural gas to highway maintenance to job training for people on welfare. It is very likely that they will try to sell off public and non-profit housing.

Why Do We Think the Socreds are Serious About This?

(a) We have a copy of the September 1987 Social Services and Housing three-year plan which includes a note to "increase the capacity for self directed purchase housing." This means that the government plans to sell off public and non-profit housing.

(b) The Socreds have been selling off "pieces" of the social housing system since 1987. In 1987 they privatized all of the contracts for building and maintaining social housing. In 1987, the B.C. Housing Management Commission building of the new social housing units was tendered to the most competitive bidder. It is important to remember that a government can privatize much of a public operation and still call it part of the public sector.

Margaret Mitchell, president of the Vancouver and District Tenants Association, has been advocating for more real *public* housing. The Vancouver and District Tenants Association wants to see 125,000 public housing units in B.C., not just the meagre 10,000 that exist now. There hasn't been any public housing built since 1979, the same year that Thatcher started privatizing in Britain.

(c) Mitchell received a letter from Claude Richmond stating: "If privatizing social housing is the most cost effective method of

managing social housing, then we will pursue it" (September 1987).

d) On February 7, Claude Richmond appointed a new chairman for BCHMC. Peter Thomas has taken over the helm. Peter Thomas has written such books as *The Art of Selling*, *The Joy of Selling*, and *21 Steps to Successful Selling*. He is chairman of the board of Century 21 Real Estate. He is associated with Nelson Skalbania. He believes in the "gospel of salesmanship." He wants to encourage the private sector. He wants to try innovative approaches to social housing. He was previously the chairman of the B.C. government's Privatization Review Committee. Does it look like the Socreds are pursuing privatization?

(e) We know that Intergovernmental Relations Minister Stephen Rogers went to England to study Thatcher's privatization program and is being advised by bankers and investors that were instrumental in Maggie's privatization scheme. In 1987, Rogers attended a privatization conference in Vancouver. He said that B.C. is willing to show "leadership" in privatization in Canada. He said, "Thank god for Thatcher or nobody would be doing it."

(f) The Socreds are privatizing land in other areas. The Expo lands and Crown land in the Coquitlam area are two examples.

What Will be Their Sneaky Strategy to Sell Off Public Housing?

Stephen Rogers favours Madsen Pirie's approach to privatization. Pirie is featured speaker at conferences on privatization sponsored by the right-wing National Citizens' Coalition. Pirie managed to sell off most of Britain's public assets. These assets took over 100 years to accumulate, and less than 10 years to get rid of almost entirely. In 1978 England had the most public assets in the world; by 1990 he says that it will have the fewest public assets.

That's his motto: GET RID OF IT. Sell it piece by piece, sell it wholesale, but GET RID OF IT. He says that each country, like Canada, will have its own quirks, and it takes work to get a good strategy that people will buy. But, according to a report on the Fraser Institute's conference on privatization, there are three guiding principles. Here's what they are, and how the Socreds will probably use them.

1. Make Friends of Your Enemies

Buy off the public. Find out who the public interest groups are and make them a deal that they can't refuse. The Vancouver and District Tenants Association is a likely target.

The Socreds might offer to sell the property and housing units to the present tenants, or to other individual members of the public. They might offer to sell it to you share by share, at a reduced rate, so that you will make a quick instant profit. They will say that this is "your opportunity to own your own home." They will say that they are offering you a chance at "the pride of ownership." They might offer to sell your home to you at a price below market rate, and even guarantee "preferential credit" to ensure mortgage rates below your present rent.

Say you do buy a house from Social Services and Housing. In

case you haven't noticed, most "happy homeowners" in Vancouver who are low or middle income, can no longer afford to own their own homes. They have to take in renters, not out of the good of their hearts, but to cover costs. Many are forced to sell their home of many years, and leave Vancouver. Who buys their homes? Realty companies, investors, *not* average people.

The only hope you have for long-term security is getting the government to EXPAND public housing, not "get rid of it." Once the Socreds finish with selling public housing, it will be impossible for any future government to buy it back. The "shares" will be too widely dispersed. Pirie says: "When the opposition gets in, they will not be able to get back those houses... They are going to have to accept the new status quo."

2. Identify All of the Objections and Disarm Them

The Socreds know that we will resist privatization. They know that not everybody agrees that the only motive for life is sheer profit. They know that we do not agree that some people should have homes, while others sleep in the streets. They know that if they sell off public housing, they will have succeeded in beginning the dismantling of B.C.'s society. Next to go will be GAIN, health care, and education. They know that most decent Canadians don't like this.

But if the Socreds follow Pirie's strategy, they will be ready for us. If we say: "But what about the people who will go homeless? What about the increased gap between the rich and the poor?" They will guarantee new homes. They will cite "home ownership" as closing the gap. They will offer us any answer that we want. They do not have to follow through with any of this, they just have to make the public believe that they will. But a public "high" on quick profits from shares and short-term profit is easy to buy.

3. Privatize the Process of Privatization

This means that government should contract out the implementation of privatization. That way, the government is not held accountable. The Socreds are already doing this. They have privatized the architects, builders, and to a large extent the management of public housing. Their last step is to do the actual selling of our homes.

What's Been Happening in England?

In England, residents were in for a rude surprise after privatization. Here's some of the things that happened there that could happen here:

First, only some of the tenants will be able to afford to buy, no matter what the conditions. You might be given only a couple of weeks to decide if you want to buy. If you don't, the offer will go to an outsider. Those that can't or don't want to buy will either be evicted, or will have to pay rent to a new "private" landlord.

There is no guarantee that these new landlords will keep rents low, maintain repairs, etc. Tenants lose long-term security to their homes, yet Peter Thomas and his boys will try to make you believe that all that you have to gain is long-term security: "a home to pass on to your grandchildren."

Those poor who are evicted will have no place to go. In England, entire families are living on the streets, squatting, and staying in dingy hotel rooms. Maggie paints a picture of happy homeowners. She forgets to finish the equation: happy homeowners at the expense of thousands of "new" homeless.

Long-term security is NOT possible in the marketplace or the private sector. The marketplace is based on wheeling, dealing, and eventually buying the little person out.

How Can We Fight to Keep Public Housing?

(1) Make sure all tenants understand what is happening in Britain, how the privatizers use sneaky words and phrases to get support for their scheme, and how tenants lose in the long term.

(2) Make the public aware of the long-term implications: thousands of B.C. residents will be homeless if they have to depend on market housing.

(3) Educate the public to realize that privatization is not security, but the insecurity of the marketplace in all aspects of our lives. Explain that selling public housing actually increases homelessness and the gap between the rich and poor. Explain that once the houses are gone, there is no getting them back. Ask people:

"Is this the 'secure' future you want for your grandchildren?"

4) We suspect that the Socreds are preparing NOW to sell housing. They will probably want to get some of it done before the next election, to bask in the short-term "success" of those who are seduced by Peter the Wolf. They will get re-elected, and when the long-term results come down, they will no longer be accountable. We *must* GET RID OF the Socreds. To the Socreds, the business of government IS business. Vote for a government with commitment to long-term security.

5) It is no coincidence that free trade is here. Privatization IS the American Way.

6) Don't fall for any of their ploys. Just remember: privatization means some short-term gains for some, long-term disaster for many while rich investors prosper, and the dismantling of our society.

7) Develop a plan of action such as leafleting, board meetings about this issue, support from other groups, maybe lawn signs saying: This house is not for sale!

Beware of Phony Offers from Peter Thomas

According to *Equity* magazine, Peter Thomas "gets $10,000 a day for explaining to others the joys of 'hot button selling.' Thomas is always selling and that makes it hard to get a fix on what is going on inside his head. Is he telling you something because he wants to say it or because he thinks you want to hear it?" Need I say more?

Prepared for End Legislated Poverty, February 15, 1989.
(Quotes from Madsen Pirie are from a luncheon speech that he gave to the National Citizens' Coalition.)

Solutions from the Community

Only a partnership of six related groups will provide practical solutions...The six-group partnership must include:

a) the homeless themselves, to identify needs, expectations and aspirations;

b) the volunteer and local charitable organizations with extensive pioneer experience in providing shelter and urgent health and food services for the poor;

c) private industry providing investment, contracting and building services;

d) the municipalities and local government who influence location and availability of land and buildings for housing projects, while being responsible for establishing norms and regulations through local by-laws and ordinances;

e) the provinces and their agencies who have the Canadian constitutional jurisdiction for housing and social services. The provinces represent a major source of policy initiatives and the critical opportunity for coordinating the delivery of health and social services to the homeless in relation to shelter provision and appropriate accommodation;

f) the federal government is, through its taxation power, able to raise and allocate appropriate resources to housing and social services programmes including social housing on a national basis.

> from "Shelter Or Homes?" by H. Peter Oberlander and Arthur L. Fallick

Homeless Persons Outreach Project

The Homeless Persons Outreach Project in Toronto was established to make contact with, and hear the opinions of, the poor and homeless of Toronto. In fall 1989, the eight members of the Homeless Persons Outreach Group held meetings at nine locations—a mix of hostels and drop-ins—to hear what the users thought, what they liked and didn't like about Toronto, and what were their suggestions for Toronto's future development. Here are some of those suggestions:

More rights for roomers.

More public toilets and drinking fountains.

Provide better chances for people who only have a few years of job experience, when the want ads all ask for a whole lot more.

Clean up burned out buildings right away so new housing can be built and the people that lived there for a long time are not left homeless.

Scatter low income housing throughout the City.

We are all one City—change the way people feel and talk about the division between the haves and the have-nots—make all parts of the city good places to live, not just some of them, like Rosedale.

Get a place where I can get along with my landlord.

More low rental or Ontario Housing—when a woman is being battered, they should move in and say he should move out and let the woman move back in.

I'd like to see a rooming house for recovering alcoholics—pay your own rent, the superintendent will know something about alcoholism. Permanent for as long as you want, somebody to talk to, you don't have to be there for meals.

More security in housing.

Social assistance for homeless people/More money for social assistance recipients.

More control over quality of rental rooms—inspections.

More homes for native people, should have first priority, they were here first.

More public baths and delousing facilities.

More opportunities to speak out like this: we can speak for ourselves, we don't need people to speak for us.

Would buy as many houses as possible and turn them all into drop-ins.

Eliminate need to have drop-ins (i.e., All have money and security and a place to be).

Provide more shelters for runaways and workers to help them.

Build low-rental housing, so everyone—both rich and poor—can get work and a place to live in the City.

Build affordable housing as the main thing. When you pay $800 per month rent and you're only making $1000 per month, you only have $200 per month left for food, transportation and everything else.

More native street counsellors, judges, police, politicians and civil servants.

Better ways of sharing housing in regions outside of Metro. Choices for people who want to live there.

Have someone who assesses housing and doesn't let people live in dumps—standards of a place to fit the costs.

Stiff penalties for landlords who evict in winter.

More lay people sitting on committees to see where government funds go: municipal, federal, provincial.

I like it when street people can take control and have input.

Emergency service to go out and pick up handicapped people who are sleeping in shelters.

Employ homeless people to help homeless people. Any seven men in this room would do a better job of getting people out of the welfare system than most social workers.

Start an awareness program across Canada because people are blind to homelessness.

More homes for the homeless.

(More details of the project and its findings have been published in *Homeless, but not helpless*, available from the Healthy City Office, 219-40 Dundas Street West, Toronto, ON M5G 2C2.)

Co-op Housing
by Stephen Learey, DERA

"What we do is work on housing where people have to live together. We don't have the supervisory staff to deal with people who have problems. When it comes to people with substance abuse, mental problems, we don't claim to house people like that. It's hard enough getting the staff for just a normal building. What we want is a nice community of people. If there is someone with substance abuse, the tenants will say they want that person out. We have buildings that have Chinese and non-Chinese, and anyone that has a racial bias will not get in. We have tenant committees set up in the buildings so that we can hear about the problems that are going on.

"The Four Sisters [Housing Co-op] has probably the highest rate of subsidized people in any Vancouver co-op. Sixty to seventy percent of the people are subsidized. There are the people who are paying low end of market. Then the people that are paying maximum rent—they are subsidized a little too. We set a bachelor suite at the welfare rate, yet there are other places that set them above the welfare rate. Even in our community here we have co-ops that charge more, and people have to take their rent out of their food money. The way the Four Sisters works, DERA initiated it, but once the co-op is built, the members take over the subsidy rate.

"The seniors' housing, the non-profit housing we've built in the last few years, everyone in the building is subsidized. A single person can't earn in excess of $17,000. The selection process is: tenants interview the people. They give them a yes or a no. Then we look at things like age, are they living in a hotel, etc. Like, a priority is if someone is already in social housing, things like that. Of any social housing built in this community, we have by far the most. Certain housing in this community excluded downtown eastside people because they say they are too much of a problem.

"Most co-op housing is share purchase. This creates a problem for poor people—you need $1500 before you can move in. If you are on welfare it's a problem. Sometimes you can get a low-interest loan, but you still have to pay it back out of your cheque. Our co-ops just ask a half a month's rent. It's the only co-op that does this. People don't have to go into debt. They can get the half month's deposit from welfare. We have about 2600 people on an up-to-date waiting list.

"We get requests for help from Victoria, Coquitlam, all over. We give out advice freely. We do have difficulty in teaching all aspects of housing. We have a very small staff ourselves, to do the housing we want to do. We are stretched. We wouldn't turn anyone down from the community. In fact, if they didn't want to deal with us, we would refer them. We didn't have any skills in the beginning. We had to find out the hard way. We had to go with other groups who were professional at it, who taught us a lot."

CEEDS

by Ben Noir

The beautiful rolling ranchland of British Columbia's vast Cariboo region is a joy to behold, but living can get pretty tough in winter if you haven't got a regular roof over your head and a warm stove nearby.

A group of organic farmers in the Cariboo are providing their own collective solution to homelessness in what is one of North America's last bastions of so-called rugged individualism. It involves joining the rural life, becoming attuned to the regular cycles of nature, and being willing to live as part of a group of friends and co-workers.

A regular regimen of feeding the pigs and hoeing the turnips is a healthy alternative to the stresses and dangers of modern life in industrialized society, according to the Cariboo Community Enhancement and Economic Development Society (CEEDS).

CEEDS operates four farms and two market gardens in the Cariboo. In its 15 years of existence, the non-profit society has provided safe, free shelter to hundreds of people who had nowhere else to go. Many of the homeless were native Indians displaced from their reserves to the towns of the Cariboo, and caught in the treadmill of welfare and alcohol. Known as "troopers," the native street people often have no regular homes, surviving in tents and shacks on the outskirts of communities like Williams Lake and 100 Mile House. For a few days, weeks, or months at a time, the troopers can get a break from town, eating nutritious food and getting regular exercise in farm chores. Everybody who lives at the CEEDS farms takes part in activities as they are able.

At one time, CEEDS also ran a hostel in Williams Lake. On cold nights, with the temperature dropping past 40 degrees below zero, people were lodged in every nook and cranny, covering all floor space. But local authorities, who had done nothing to deal

A cabin on one of the CEEDS farms in the Cariboo

with the problem of homelessness, harassed the facility until it had to close.

Since 1989, CEEDS has developed a relationship with the Carnegie Centre, in Vancouver's Downtown Eastside. Dozens of low-income city people have visited the farms; some have stayed for months.

CEEDS is not connected to any religious or political group. Its primary goal is to produce healthy, organically grown food, and to provide a model of community living that is ecologically sound and fulfilling for all members. For more information on CEEDS, write them at Box 5, Buhl Site, RR 1, 100 Mile House, BC V0K 2E0; or call (604) 395-4225.

It breaks my heart to drive down Dunbar and Granville and see all those single-storey shops when land is the big expense in housing. Why couldn't the government give low-interest loans to store owners to build suites above their stores?
    May Gutteridge, St James Social Service Society; quoted in "The Homeless" by Moira Farrow, Western Living, *April 1990.*

SOLUTIONS FROM THE COMMUNITY

Since [homelessness] is inextricably linked to the combined effects of poverty, inadequate income, inaffordable or substandard housing, lack of meaningful employment opportunities, inadequate social benefits, deinstitutionalization, urban change and the differential standards which society seems to be willing to tolerate for some of its members, explanation of the causes, and by implication, the selection of practical solutions, requires comprehensive, multi-dimensional analyses which go beyond single factor causal explanations.

from "Shelter or Homes: A Contribution to the Search for Solutions to Homelessness in Canada" by H. Peter Oberlander and Arthur L. Fallick, from the Centre for Human Settlements, UBC. This booklet includes information on four projects, representative examples of solutions to homelessness currently being tested in Canada. These are: 310 Alexander Street, Vancouver B.C., 90 Shuter Street, Toronto Ont., Auberge Communautaire du Sud-Ouest, Montreal, Que., and 506 Bronson, Ottawa, Ont.

We tend to view housing as a consumer item to be purchased by those who can afford it or as an investment option to maximize profit. In responding to the homeless, we have tended to offer short-term shelter at minimal cost. Without a shift in our values regarding housing, homelessness will persist as a social phenomenon and we can expect further increases in the numbers of homeless men and women in our cities. To counteract this trend, housing should be considered a basic right. 'Housing' should also be understood to mean more than simple shelter... With long-term, supportive housing, individuals are better able to cope with personal problems, to make appropriate use of support services, and to decrease or even eliminate their dependency on the social service system.

from "The Case for Long-Term, Supportive Housing," Single Displaced Persons' Project.

Consider where we would be as a society if we treated education and health care in the way we treat housing. I think we would be pretty dumb and sickly! Last century we defined education as a right—people under a certain age had

a right to a good quality, free education; education became a right and a priority. In this century, health care became a right and a priority, and now all people have a right to good quality health care.
> from "Housing and Homelessness" by David Hulchanski, in A Place to Call Home.

Homelessness: What won't stop it and what will?
by Jean Swanson

In some countries, housing is considered a right. A person or family can rent an apartment for 5 to 10 percent of their monthly income. In Vancouver today, housing does not seem to be a right. Thousands of low income people pay 50 to 70 percent of their income on housing. Developers and landlords seem to think that they have a right to more and more profits. These people see buying, selling, and flipping housing as their ticket to riches. They think that their right to buy, sell, and flip is more important than our right to a secure roof over our heads. Some governments stick up for the developers and landlords. They refuse to pass laws that help low-income people and homeless people.

Blaming homeless people for their lack of housing will not stop homelessness. Many stories about the homeless that appear in the corporate-owned media imply or state that people are homeless because they are alcoholics, or because they are mentally ill. But a civilized society would recognize that sick people need extra help in getting housing and would provide that help.

Feeling guilty about homelessness will not end it. Donating to charities for the homeless will not end homelessness. Setting up counselling programs for the homeless will not end homelessness.

The best way to help the homeless is to vote for politicians who will pass laws to prevent homelessness.

We need action at all three levels of government if Canada is to prevent homelessness. In Vancouver, the Tenants Rights Coalition has developed a 13-step solution to the housing crisis. If poli-

SOLUTIONS FROM THE COMMUNITY

ticians acted on these 13 points, we would not have homeless people in Canada.

Protecting Tenants

1. A fair rent review system requiring landlords to justify rent increases on the basis of increased operating costs.
2. Longer timelines for eviction for landlord use or redevelopment of property, with full relocation costs borne by the owner.
3. Provincial Rental Housing Protection Act allowing demolition of affordable rental housing only where a developer provides an equal number of affordable housing units or contributes to a social housing replacement fund.
4. Increased pensions and welfare rates reflecting current rents.

Saving Affordable Housing

5. City moratorium on conversions from rental housing to condominiums.
6. City moratorium on demolition of affordable rental housing until provincial protections are in place.
7. Speculation tax on profits from flipping property, with exemption for long-time owners—tax revenues to be used as part of a social housing replacement fund.
8. Equitable system of property taxes to protect low- and middle-income homeowners.
9. Municipal, provincial, and federal funds to help upgrade existing affordable housing, particularly basement suites.

Creating New Affordable Housing

10. Funding for 20,000 new social housing units in Greater Vancouver, as an immediate short-term goal, suitable to a range of groups including seniors, disabled, single parents, and those with special needs, provided through a range of social housing alternatives including public housing, non-profit housing, and co-op housing.
11. Municipal, provincial, and federal land-banking to provide free or subsidized land for public, non-profit, and co-op housing.
12. City policy forcing mega-project developers to provide free land for social housing, paid for out of the profits made from rezoning.
13. Re-establishment of the local area planning process and

development of long-term affordable housing plans with full community and citizen input.

Election Agenda on Canadian Housing August 1988

This position paper was prepared by representatives of six groups involved with housing and poverty. The six groups are: Urban Core Support Network; National Anti-Poverty Organization; Canadian Housing and Renewal Association; Centre for Equality Rights in Accommodation; National Action Committee on the Status of Women; and the Co-operative Housing Foundation of Canada.

The federal government must renew its commitment to the provision of housing to the half-million Canadians currently without adequate, affordable housing. Its involvement and leadership are critical to meeting the needs of these Canadians. There is growing evidence, however, that the federal government has been abdicating its leadership role in housing, and has been devolving responsibility for the provision of affordable housing increasingly to the provincial jurisdiction.

In 1987, the International Year of Shelter for the Homeless, the United Nations articulated the right of all individuals to:
- a real home—one which provides protection from the elements; has access to safe water and sanitation; provides for secure tenure and personal safety; is within easy reach of centres for employment, education and health care; and is at a cost which people and society can afford.

To make the Canadian government's commitment to this right real, the Election Agenda on Canadian Housing is calling on it to:
- entrench the right to decent housing without discrimination;
- adopt a "housing first" policy for the disposition of surplus lands and buildings owned by the federal government, Crown corporations, and federal agencies;
- increase the level of production of non-profit and co-operative housing so that these units comprise one-half of all rental housing starts in Canada.

Entrenchment of the right to decent housing, without discrimination:
BACKGROUND: More than half a million Canadian households

currently live without decent housing, and the number is increasing.

Discrimination in housing against disadvantaged groups (including low-income people, families with children, social assistance recipients, visible minorities, women, disabled persons, and Native people) has become so widespread that affordable and appropriate housing is rarely available to those with the most limited incomes and the greatest need.

SOLUTION: The right to adequate housing should be entrenched in the Canadian Charter of Rights and Freedoms, by including in the right to security of the person (contained in Section 7 of the Charter) those rights enshrined in the 1948 Universal Declaration of Human Rights adopted by the United Nations:

> Everyone has the right to a standard of living adequate for health and well-being...including food, clothing, housing and medical care and necessary social services.

In addition, the federal government should make federal transfer payments contingent on the inclusion in all provincial Human Rights Codes of a prohibition against discrimination in housing because of family composition or age, level or source of income, pregnancy, gender, disability, sexual orientation and race. This would ensure provincial compliance with the equality provision of the Charter (Sections 15 and 23).

COSTS: Prohibiting discrimination against disadvantaged people encourages a more economical and rational distribution of existing housing stock by ensuring that affordable housing is available to those most in need. Entrenchment of the right to adequate housing is therefore a benefit rather than a cost. As well, this entrenchment will lead to significant preventative savings in health and social services, and in the long-term social costs of inadequate housing.

Adoption of a 'housing first' policy for the disposition of surplus lands and buildings in the federal jurisdiction:
BACKGROUND: Housing market conditions are making it increasingly difficult to develop housing for low- and modest-income earners. Land costs are so high in some areas that producers of non-profit and co-operative housing cannot afford to purchase potential sites held by private owners. Access to land is one of the most critical barriers to producing affordable housing today.

SOLUTION: The adoption of a "housing first" policy would require the federal government to offer first to non-profit and co-operative providers of affordable housing any land or buildings within its control or ownership and available for disposal. The price of the land must not exceed the amount permitted under non-profit and co-operative housing programs. In this way, housing could be provided in areas of high demand where land costs have severely restricted development opportunities. As well, publicly owned land is often on relatively large sites, and is frequently situated in locations that are otherwise out of financial reach of non-profit and co-operative housing groups. The development of such sites could involve interested local residents and groups in the design and planning of these new communities.

COSTS: The expeditious sale of federal lands at below-market prices would provide an immediate cash benefit to the government and would enable construction of some affordable housing units without increases in per-unit costs and subsidies required under the non-profit and co-operative housing programs.

Increase in the level of production of non-profit and co-operative housing so that these units comprise one half of all rental housing starts in Canada

BACKGROUND: During the United Nations' International Year of Shelter for the Homeless (1987), the lack of affordable, decent housing in Canada was documented in more than one study. An estimated half-million Canadian families are living in inadequate shelter, many without any accommodation at all.

More federal tax expenditures and benefits subsidize private ownership than go to assist those in need of affordable rental housing.

The federal government currently funds approximately 19,000 units of co-operative and non-profit housing per year. An advisory committee to the Government of Ontario recently estimated that the production of 14,000 units is needed to meet the crisis in Toronto alone.

SOLUTION: Approximately 200,000 units of housing are produced in Canada each year; of these, it is estimated that 40 percent, or 80,000, are rental housing units. One-half of these, or 40,000, should be produced by non-profit and co-operative housing corporations. In this way, Canada would target *20 percent* of all its new housing stock for those least able to afford appropriate housing through the private sector.

This solution would result in stable communities, could increase participation in the labour force by individuals with stable accommodation, and would maintain high employment in the construction industry.

COSTS: To increase the annual production of social housing units to 40,000, the federal government's expenditure would have to increase by less than one-tenth of one percent of the federal budget, or less than $60 million. Government expenditures on private homeownership through the tax system are estimated to be more than $3 billion, and are not targeted to Canadians most in need.

The costs of not dealing with the growing problem of inadequate and unaffordable housing are high. Shelters, hotels and hospitals are expensive to build, to maintain and to operate; the cost of one night in a hospital could well equal a month's rent in a permanent social housing unit. While social costs cannot be measured as easily, the effect of unstable and inadequate living arrangements has been well documented in large American cities, as have the health problems resulting from homelessness.

Vancouver Solutions

These are some of the solutions I heard over and over again as I interviewed people on the streets of Vancouver.

Teach us how to get funding for special housing, how to set up housing for special needs people (HIV positive). Houses could be renovated. We could take over ownership—*John Turvey, DEYAS.*

Social housing on a small scale—10 or fewer people—for the mentally sick, with some supervision depending on the tenants' problems—*street nurses.*

A safe shelter where runaway kids will not be apprehended, with a 48-hour time-out, where they would be listened to.

We must change the attitude that it's okay for people (women, children, and men) to give sex in return for shelter. We must provide options.

Homeless families must be placed in decent housing, a safe environment—not in skid row hotels.

For every unit lost, one must be replaced.

Illegal suites should be legal.

Protect what we've got instead of allowing closures.

Welfare and minimum wage must become "real" so there's enough money to provide shelter, food.

Listen to the people who are on the front line, people who work with the homeless.

So people start opening their god-darn eyes, start looking around them, and have a little more kindness and consideration in their heart—*Melissa*.

The marketplace must not control our right to a home.

Give tenants security of tenure.

Stop raising rents.

Vote for politicians who will find solutions to homelessness.

Stop blaming the victim.

Karen O'Shannacery, Lookout

"We have had both men and women recover. In fact, we had a marriage at Lookout. Remember, Lookout is the place for people to stay who have been written off by and large by everybody else. So we have a fellow who's in a wheelchair, and a woman who's mentally handicapped, and once they were stabilized and given the support they needed, the appropriate services, they were able to maintain, and they fell in love, they had a two-year courtship, surmounting all odds because everybody tried to tell these people *not* to have anything to do with each other. They were homeless when they came to us, but you give them their pride, give them their dignity...

"The marriage took place about a year and a half ago, and they haven't been back since. They send us notes every now and then, telling us how great they're making out."

Epilogue

A black woman came into the Carnegie Centre. When she spoke, she sounded just like I used to sound. Her name was Althea, and she was from East London, England, a literacy tutor here for a conference.

She wanted a copy of my book, and we became good friends, exchanging addresses, spending time together.

There was still one part of my homelessness that I had to deal with, and I felt I was now ready to face it. I told Althea that I had come to Canada as an immigrant when I was 23, with my husband and child. I had lost touch with all my relatives there, running away, not looking back, avoiding the pain. Althea said she would look up my family, see if there were any uncles, aunts, or cousins living in the East End of London. I thought perhaps my father, Walter Swann, could even be alive.

I have never been back to my birth land. Homelessness doesn't always involve shelter; homelessness can also mean that you don't feel you belong anywhere. Many people have told me this.

Althea told me that housing is a real mess in London (it was a mess when I was there too). She told me about Thatcher's plan to privatize social housing, and gave me an example. Anne, a single mother with three children, lives in social (council) housing. Rent is £126 a month. If Anne were to buy her flat, she would need 100 percent mortgage; this would be £400 per month. Also there would be the cost of repairs, taxes, and the threat of interest increases. She just can't find the money. If her housing is privatized, she will have to pay rent at marketplace values, which she can't afford either.

On top of that there is the new poll tax. Everyone has to pay it. Anne has to pay £474 a year; she doesn't know where she will find the money. If a person lives in an area which is poor, and there are many needs—like daycare—the poll tax is higher. If a rich man owns six homes in the area, he only pays one poll tax, and it is the same amount as what Anne pays. (In Spring 1991 the poll tax was abolished.)

There is not a lot of housing being built in England these days, so the government spends millions of dollars to place homeless families in hotel rooms or bed-and-breakfast places, which are crowded and seldom adequate.

This book I have written on homelessness is just the tip of the iceberg. These stories, interviews, observations are an intimate look at homelessness. People in this book are real, not just statistics. They are as I see them and hear them; their thoughts are unedited by me. Their voices are their own. It's a patchwork of all colours, sizes, and depths. I've put them together in this book the same way you quilt a quilt. This is not a scientific study, just the simple truth as it happens. The information from other provinces and the U.S. is here as a reminder that homelessness is universal and is mostly a question of poverty.

For nine months I have kept company with you, the reader. It's now time for us to part. I will continue to document homelessness, perhaps some readers will find it in their hearts to help create a political will to implement solutions to homelessness.

Bibliography

The following are the main books that I used in my research on homelessness, the ones I actually mentioned or quoted from in my book. I've listed author(s), title, and included an ordering address or publisher.

Fallick, Arthur L., general editor. *A Place to Call Home: A Conference on Homelessness in British Columbia.* Centre for Human Settlements, Faculty of Graduate Studies, University of British Columbia, Vancouver, B.C. V6T 1W5. 1987.

Goldberg, Michael. *Closing the Gap: A Comparison Between the Costs of Daily Living and Income Assistance Rates in British Columbia.* Social Planning and Research Council, 106-2182 West 12th Avenue, Vancouver, B.C. V6K 2N4. 1990.

Homeless Persons Outreach Project. *Homeless, not helpless.* Healthy City Office, 219-40 Dundas Street West, Toronto, Ont. M5G 2C2. 1990.

Hulchanski, J.D. *Who Are the Homeless? What is Homelessness? The Politics of Defining an Emerging Policy Issue.* School of Community and Regional Planning, 6333 Memorial Road, University of British Columbia, Vancouver, B.C. V6T 1W5. 1987.

Lang-Runtz, Heather and Doyne C. Ahem, editors. *New Partnerships —Building For the Future* (Proceedings of the Canadian Conference to Observe the International Year of Shelter for the Homeless). Canadian Association of Housing and Renewal Officials, #1 - 20 Rochester Street, Ottawa, Ont. K1R 7V3. 1988.

McLaughlin, Mary Ann. *Homelessness in Canada: The Report of the National Inquiry.* Canadian Council on Social Development, 55 Parkdale Avenue, P.O. Box 3505, Station C, Ottawa, Ont. K1Y 4G1. 1989.

Oberlander, H. Peter and Arthur L. Fallick. *Shelter or Homes? A Contribution to the Search for Solutions to Homelessness in Canada.*

Centre for Human Settlements, Faculty of Graduate Studies, University of British Columbia, Vancouver, B.C. V6T 1W5. 1987.

Oberlander, H. Peter and Arthur L. Fallick. *Homelessness and the Homeless: Responses and Innovations.* Centre for Human Settlements, Faculty of Graduate Studies, University of British Columbia, Vancouver, B.C. V6T 1W5. 1988.

Pinsky, Barry and Mitzi D'Sousa. *Catalogue of Canadian Housing and Shelter Organizations.* Rooftops Canada Foundation, 100 - 22 Mowat Avenue, Toronto, Ont. M6K 3E8. 1988.

Radford, Joyce L., Alan J.C. King and Wendy K. Warren. *Street Youth and AIDS.* Federal Centre for AIDS, Health Protection Branch, Health and Welfare Canada, 301 Elgin Street, Ottawa, Ont. K1A 0L2. 1989.

Reyes, Lilia M. and Laura DeKoven Waxman. *A Status Report on Hunger and Homelessness in America's Cities: 1989.* U.S. Conference of Mayors, 1620 Eye Street NW, Washington, D.C. 20006. 1989.

Resources

When I decided to include a cross-Canada list of resources in this book, I thought it would be easy. I thought I'd just call up one of the local housing groups, TRAC or DERA, or even End Legislated Poverty, and they'd have a ready-made list for me to include.

It was not that easy.

There are hundreds, maybe even thousands of groups all across the country, in cities and small towns. Groups that run shelters, transition houses; groups that fund and build housing for low-income people; groups that provide legal information and advocacy services, that help tenants fight illegal evictions and rent increases. I got lists from a variety of sources, and all the lists had different names on them!

What I decided to do was list one or two groups for each province, or for the major cities in each province. I've tried to have an anti-poverty group and/or a group that focuses on housing issues. If you contact the group listed for your province or city below, I think they'll be able to help you, or will be able to refer you to a local service or group that *can* help.

It's not ideal, as I realize people on low-income, or people facing the stress of a rent increase or an eviction do not have lots of time or money for phone calls. But I hope that this resource list proves to be of some help. And if there's not a group listed for your community, try the phone book first. See if there's a local women's centre, or an anti-poverty group, or any kind of crisis line.

GOOD LUCK!

(Also included in this list are all the groups or resources I've referred to in this book, as well as the organizations that helped me compile the list. Thanks to all of you!)

NEWFOUNDLAND

Social Action Office
Box 986
St. John's, Nfld   A1C 5M3
709-739-6178

NOVA SCOTIA

Cornerstone Housing Society
5663 Cornwallis Street
Halifax, NS   B3K 1B6
902-420-0226

Halifax Metro Welfare Rights Association
5571 Cunard Street
Halifax, NS   B3K 1C5
902-422-6424

NEW BRUNSWICK

Fredericton Anti-Poverty Organization
120 King Street
Fredericton, NB   E3B 1C9
506-458-9102

Housing Alternatives
61 Union Street, La Tour Terrace
St. John, NB   E2L 1A2
506-632-9393

QUEBEC

Welfare Rights
707-75 Avenue, Room 4
La Salle, PQ   H8R 3Y2
514-595-7305

Chez Doris
2696 ouest, boulevard de Maisonneuve
Montreal, PQ   H3T 1N3
514-937-2341

FRAPRU (Front d'Action Populaire Reamenagement Urbain)/PROUD (People's Rights Over Urban Development)
1212 Panet Street, £318
Montreal, PQ   H2L 2Y7
514-522-1010

Maison Marguerite
1183 Rue St Mahier
Montreal, PQ   H3H 2P7
514-932-2250

ONTARIO

Canadian Council on Social Development
55 Parkdale Avenue
P.O. Box 3505, Station C
Ottawa, ON   K1Y 4G1
613-728-1865

Canadian Housing Information Centre
Canadian Mortgage and Housing Commission
682 Montreal Road
Ottawa, ON   K2A 0P7
613-748-2367

Cooperative Housing Foundation
275 Bank Street, Suite 202
Ottawa, ON   K2P 2L6
613-238-4644

Federation of Ottawa-Carlton Tenants Association
Box 3347, Station D
Ottawa, ON   K1P 8H5
613-594-5429

Housing Help
792 Somerset Street West
Ottawa, ON   K1R 6R2
613-563-4532

RESOURCES

**National Anti-Poverty
Organization**
456 Rideau Street
Ottawa, ON   K1N 5Z4
613-234-3332

**Regional Municipality of
Ottawa/Carleton Social
Services Department**
495 Richmond Road
Ottawa, ON   K2A 0G3
613-728-3913
613-560-1335 (after hours
 emergency)

Basic Poverty Action Group
c/o The Meeting Place
761 Queen Street West
Toronto, ON   M6J 1G1
416-366-3571

Homes First
393 Front Street East, 2nd Floor
Toronto, ON   M5A 1G4
416-362-2827

**Metro Toronto Tenants
Association**
344 Bloor Street West, Suite 403
Toronto, ON   M5S 3A7
416-921-8583

**Ontario Coalition Against
Poverty**
249 Sherbourne Street
Toronto, ON   M5A 2R9
416-925-6939

Shelter for the Homeless
22 Mowat Avenue, Suite 100
Toronto, ON   M6K 3E8
416-538-7511

United Tenants of Ontario
c/o 720 Spadina Avenue, Suite
 410
Toronto, ON   M5S 2T9
416-363-8866

Urban Core Support Network
315 Dundas East
Toronto, ON   M5A 2A2
416-363-7655

MANITOBA

Main Street Project
75 Martha Street
Winnipeg, MB   R3B 1A4
204-942-0434

**Manitoba Anti-Poverty
Organization**
365 McGee Street
Winnipeg, MB   R3G 3M5
204-786-3323

SASKATCHEWAN

The Circle Project
625 Elphinstone Street
Regina, SK   S4T 3L1
306-347-7515

Community Housing Worker
Urban Planning Department
2476 Victoria Avenue
Box 1790
Regina, SK   S4P 3C8
306-777-7534

**Saskatchewan Anti-Poverty
Legal Rights Committee**
325 Avenue E South
Saskatoon, SK   S7M 1S2
306-653-6260

ALBERTA

**Center for Income Security
and Employment Association**
650, 608-7 Street South West
Calgary, AB   T2P 1Z2
403-263-0701

Bissell Centre
10527-96 Street
Edmonton, AB   T5H 2H6
403-423-2285

Boyle Street Community Services Co-op
9720-102 Avenue
Edmonton, AB   T5G 1E7
403-424-4106

Edmonton Social Planning Council
41-9912-106 Street
Edmonton, AB   T5K 1C5
403-423-2031

Inner City Housing Society
3rd Floor, 10765-98 Street
Edmonton, AB   T5H 2P2
403-423-1339

BRITISH COLUMBIA

Carnegie Community Centre
401 Main Street
Vancouver, BC   V6A 2T7
604-665-2220

Centre for Human Settlements
2206 East Mall, UBC
Vancouver, BC   V6T 1W5
604-822-5254

City of Vancouver Social Planning Department
453 West 12 Avenue
Vancouver, BC   V5Y 1V4
604-873-7487

Crabtree Corner Daycare and Drop-in
101 East Cordova
Vancouver, BC   V6A 1K7
604-689-2808

Downtown Eastside Residents Association (DERA)
9 East Hastings
Vancouver, BC   V6A 1M9
604-682-0931

Downtown Eastside Women's Centre
44 East Cordova Street
Vancouver, BC   V6A 1K2
604-681-8480

Downtown Eastside Youth Activities Centre
(includes needle exchange, street nurses)
221 Main Street
Vancouver, BC   V6A 2S7
604-685-6561, 685-4488

End Legislated Poverty
211-456 West Broadway
Vancouver, BC   V5Y 1R3
604-879-1209

Evelyne Saller Centre
320 Alexander Street
Vancouver, BC   V6A 1C3
604-684-1318

First United Church
320 East Hastings
Vancouver, BC   V6A 1P4
604-681-8365

Lookout Emergency Aid Society
346 Alexander
Vancouver, BC   V6A 1G4
604-681-9126

Strathcona Mental Health Team
295 East Hastings
Vancouver, BC   V6A 1P2
604-253-4401

RESOURCES

Tenants' Rights Coalition
203-2250 Commercial Drive
Vancouver, BC   V59 5P9
604-255-3099

**Vancouver & District Public
 Housing Tenants' Ass'n**
12-246 East Broadway
Vancouver, BC   V4T 1W3
604-872-8648

Vancouver Housing Registry
501 East Broadway
Vancouver, BC   V5T 1X4
604-873-1313

Streetlink Emergency Shelter
1634 Store Street
Victoria, BC   V8W 1V3
604-383-1951

Victoria Cool Aid Society
469 Swift Street
Victoria, BC   V8W 1S2
604-383-1977

Index

"Adults only" rental housing. *See* Discrimination in rental housing
Affordable housing, 1, 14, 41, 42-45, 59, 78, 209; creation of, 95, 209; demolition of, 92-93, 95, 170; promises of, 95. *See also* Women's Housing Manifesto
Alvare, Alan, 30, 55
Anderson, Margaret, 152-54
Armstrong, Al, 29

Balmoral Hotel, 26
BASIC Poverty Action Group, 127n.
Baxter, Sheila, 21-25, 133, 139-40, 215
Bazerque, Pablo, 157-60, 173-74
Bill 51. *See* B.C. Residential Tenancy Act, amendments
Boarding homes, 27
Braha, Anita, 190
Briere, Elaine, 131n.
B.C. Housing Management Commission, 195, 196
B.C. Human Rights Act, 15, 177, 188, 190-91; violates Charter of Rights and Freedoms, 190
B.C. Human Rights Code: request for amendments to, 171
B.C. Human Rights Coalition, 190
B.C. Public Interest Advocacy Centre, 190
B.C. Residential Tenancy Act, 9, 30, 83, 188, 191; amendments, 29, 177, 186, 190
B.C. Social Services and Housing Act, 143
Brodsky, Gwen, 190

Brooks, Jeff, 30, 175, 179
Buckley, Ralph, 26-28
Burgess, A.W., 174n.
Burgess, Austin and Associates, 51

"Campbell, God," *see* Campbell, Gordon
Campbell, Gordon, 59, 70, 95, 118, 162; "38 initiatives" for "a tight housing market," 95
Canadian Council on Social Development: definition of homelessness, 127; estimate of numbers of homeless in Canada, 127
Canadian Mortgage and Housing Corporation, 14, 169; guideline 56.1, 47
Carnegie Association, 165, 167
Carnegie Centre, 99-100, 105, 116, 141, 150; programs, 99, 133, 206; staff, 99; volunteers, 100
Carnegie Library, 114
Catholic Charities, 29, 158
CEEDS (Cariboo Community Enhancement and Economic Development Society), 205-06
CERA (Centre for Equality Rights in Accommodation), Ontario, 189
Charities, 75
Chez Doris day shelter, Montreal, 2, 120, 123, 124(table)
Child advocate, 175
Child prostitution, 173
Childcare programs, 178
Chu, Keith, 80, 88n.
Chudnovsky, Rita, 175-80
Community for Creative Non-Violence, Boston, 131

224

INDEX

Conference on Homelessness in B.C., 8n.
Co-op housing 49, 50, 203-05
Cope, Audrey, 190
Cordova House, 26
Counsellors, street, 48
Covenay, Roy, 30
Crabtree Corners Drop-in and Daycare, 41, 145, 165, 176, 185
Crosswalk, 26, 29, 41, 46, 65

Davies, Libby, 118
Davies, Phil, 120
Del-Mar Hotel, 59
Demolition: of hotels and housing, 14, 16, 42, 50-51, 59, 70, 79-80, 92-93, 117, 187; recommendation of stop to, 92, 96
Demolition controls, 95
Demolition permits, 162
DERA (Downtown Eastside Residents Association) 1, 10n., 28-30, 49-51, 56, 109, 178, 185; housing, wait list, 51
Developers. *See* Real estate development; Land speculation
DEYAS (Downtown Eastside Youth Activities Society), 30, 48, 65, 150, 157, 173, 183
Discrimination, 56, 49. *See also* Racism
Discrimination in rental housing, 15-16, 35, 39, 147-48, 171, 177, 184-91, 211. *See also* Rental housing, adult only
Displacement: of longtime residents, 79
Door is Open, The, 30
Downtown eastside hotels, 26, 45, 51, 56-59, 63-70, 180-84; closure, 50, 118; and land speculation, 58; and single mothers, 39, 41, 180-89, statistics, 50; survey, 50; vacancy rate, 14. *See also* Demolition; Gentrification. *See also under* name of hotel, e.g. Balmoral, Ohio, etc.
Downtown Eastside Residents Association. *See* DERA
Downtown Eastside Youth Activities Society. *See* DEYAS
Downtown Eastside Women's Centre, 32, 35, 39, 185
Downtown Health Clinic, 30
Dunsmuir House, 30

Dugout, 30
D'Youville, Marguerite, 121-23

Earnings, average: decline in, 13
Ellaschuk, Dorothy, 114-15
Emergency shelters, 17, 40, 146 *See also under* name of shelter, e.g. Crosswalk, Lookout, Powell Place, Triage, etc.
Emergency Services, 46, 99, 140-43, 145, 154. *See also* Social Services and Housing, Ministry of
Employment trends, 14
End Legislated Poverty, 13, 56, 119
Entre Nous Femmes, 179
Evelyne Saller Centre ("44"), 114-15, 152-54, 182
Expo site, 95
Eviction, 15, 16, 29, 56, 63, 75, 109

"44", see Evelyne Saller Centre
Fallick, Arthur L., 7n., 8n., 9n., 12n., 88n., 127n., 140n., 207n.
Farrell, Tom, 29
Farrow, Moira, 51n., 206n.
Federal government housing policy. *See* Housing policy
First United Church, 30, 36, 41, 49, 55, 142, 145, 183
Fleming, Pam, 195
Fletcher, Karen, 188
Food bank, 39
Food, inexpensive, 115
Food, scarcity, 107
Food scavenging, 106-09
Foster placement, 174
Four Sisters Housing Co-op, 204
Frances Street Squatters, 72-88, 117, 145, 157; background, 72, 84; "community," 82-83; description of houses, 81; description of previous tenants, 81-82; empowerment, 74, 77, 78, 83, 87; media coverage, 83, 84, 162; philosophy, 75, 82-85; police arrest, 161-62; Squatters' Jamboree, 83; support for, 83-85; "women's only" house, 76-77. *See also* Squatters and squatting; SAVE; Yee, Ning
Fraser Institute, 197

GAIN, 39, 88; adequacy of maximum shelter allowance in meeting shelter costs, 168(table); percent-

age of clients with reported shelter costs exceeding shelter allowance by region, 166(table); percentage of income assistance recipients reporting shelter costs greater than GAIN shelter allowance, 167(table). *See also* Welfare rates
Gallagher, Karen, 137-39, 174, 184
Gastown Legal Services, 189
Gates, Rick, 175, 179
Gentrification, 49, 50, 58, 73-75, 80, 105, 162, 187; definition of, 75, 79, 85
Goldberg, Michael, 167n.
Grandview-Woodland Area Council, 84
Granville Street redevelopment, 170
Great Britain, privatization, 195-96, 199
Grey Nuns, 121. *See also* Montreal, Grey Nuns
Gutstein, Donald, 163
Gutteridge, May, 206n.

Harcourt, Mike, 118
Harrassment, 15, 17
Hartman, C., 174n.
Hays, Judy, 31
Home, definition of, 115, 171-72
Homeless people: abuse, 106; children and youth, 31, 48-49, 59, 65, 115, 150, 154, 157-58, 173-91; corporate agenda for, 126; disability rate, 126; and disease, 126; families, 182-91; HIV positive, 49, 61; and illness, 78, 100, 126; immigrants and refugees, 60, 157-59; Inuit, 125; mentally ill, 26, 27, 37, 49, 53, 55, 60, 67, 69, 115, 123, 155, 169; Natives, 146-49; single mothers, 35, 38-43, 116, 148, 182-91; sleeping out, 28-29(table), 29-31, 97, 104-07, 112, 115, 133-34, 158, 167, 169-70; speech patterns, 89; *See also* Homelessness; Montreal; Toronto; United States, homeless and homelessness; Women and abuse; World homeless, statistics
Homelessness: causes of, 1, 12-13, 100-02, 109, 128, 170, 206-07; Conference on Homelessness in B.C., 8; consequences of, 128-29; definition of, 7-11, 33, 35-36, 44, 53, 61- 62, 68, 104, 110, 127 143, 148, 152, 153, 172, 181, 183; experts on, 155; increases in, 14-17, 30, 31; and mortality rate, 126; precipitants of, 12; solutions to, 1, 33, 42-43, 90-91, 106, 111, 144, 155, 159, 172, 178, 201-16 ; statistics, 9, 26, 28-31, 44, 46, 51, 126-27, 129, 131, 171, 210; *See also* Homeless
Homeless, Interviews with. 10-11, 32-34, 35-40, 41, 56, 89-91, 98, 99-100, 103-13, 114-16, 117, 119-20, 133-35, 143-44, 145-46, 147-48, 150-52, 157, 160-61, 163-64, 165, 170-71, 181-83, 184-85, 187-88, 190, 202-03
Homeless Persons Outreach Project, Toronto, 202-03
"Hotel kids," 180-84. *See also* Homeless, children and youth; Homeless, families
Hotels, residential. *See* Downtown eastside hotels
Housing, abandonment of, 93. *See also* Frances Street Squatters; Gentrification
Housing, affordable. *See* Affordable housing
Housing, co-op. *See* Co-op housing
Housing crises, 94, 96; solutions to, 92, 96, 208-09
Housing, definition of, 207
Housing, demolition of. *See* Demolition, of hotels and housing
Housing, Low Income. *See* Affordable housing; Public housing; Social housing
Housing policy, 140
Housing, public. *See* Public housing; Social housing
Housing, public responsibility for, 41, 50
Housing, seniors'. *See* Seniors' housing
Housing, social. *See* Social housing; Public housing
Howe, Karen, 142, 183
Hulchanski, David, 8n., 88n., 140n., 187, 208n.
Human Rights Council, 191

Illegal suites. *See* Secondary suite closure
Indian Act, 149

INDEX

Interest rates, 13
Inuit homeless. *See* Homeless, Inuit

Janus, M.D., 174n.
Janzen, Cheryl, 148-49

Kilgour, Suzi, 188

Land development. *See* Real estate development
Land speculation, 118. *See also* Real estate development
Learey, Stephen, 10n., 56, 203
Leduc, Soeur Georgette, 121, 123
Long House Council of Native Ministry, 31
Lookout, 26, 28, 31, 40, 44, 47, 60, 65, 142, 159, 174, 214
Low income housing. *See* Affordable housing; Public housing; Social housing
Lucky Lodge, 105

Maison Marguerite, Montreal, 2, 121-24
MacGuire, Margot, 184-85
Marathon site, 95
Marchant, Sarah, 187-88
Marcoux, Roneen, 187
Marin, Peter, 7, 128n.
Marshall, Georgina, 145
Mavis McMullen House, 187
McCool, Carol, 189
McCormack, A., 174n.
McPhee, Betty, 41, 145, 165, 185-86
Mental illness. *See* Homeless, mentally ill
Meredith, Gail, 187
Military expenditures, 163
Minimum wage, 13, 14, 56
Ministry of Social Services and Housing. *See* Social Services and Housing, Ministry of
Ministry of Social Services and Housing Act. *See* B.C. Ministry of Social Services and Housing Act
Mitchell, Margaret, 53, 195
Mobile homes, 17
Montreal, 119-24; Chez Doris day shelter, 120, 123, 124(table); Chez Doris Annual Statistics, 124; day shelter built, 120; Grey Nuns, 121; homeless women, 120; Maison Marguerite, 121-24

Morris, Barry, 31
Mohawk Indians, Oka: Tent city in support of, 150-51
MSSH. *See* Social Services and Housing, Ministry of
Munro, Ingrid, 10n.

National Citizens' Coalition, 197
National Housing Policy, 94
Natives: and homelessness. *See* Homeless, natives
NDP, 118
Nelson, B.C., 56
New York, 85. *See also* Squatters and squatting
Nightingale, Kim, 185, 186
Noir, Ben, 205
Non-Partisan Association, 162
Nurses, street, 48, 53, 59-62

Oberlander, H. Peter, 7n., 8n., 9n., 12n., 88n., 127n., 207n.
Ohio Rooms, 26, 109
Ontario, affordable housing, loss of, 126
Ontario Ministry of Housing: budget for new housing, 126; non-profit affordable housing program statistics, 126-27
Oppenheimer Park, 158
O'Reilley, Lawrence, 29
O'Shannacery, Karen, 31, 44, 174, 214
Owl House, 146-49

Patricia Hotel, 183
Pirie, Madsen, 197, 198
Poole, Jack, 85, 86, 95; promises 2000 units of affordable housing, 95
Porter, Bruce, 189
Poverty, 13-14; and free trade, 53; government policies, 53; and mentally ill, 53; and seniors, 53; statistics, 88, 127, 140. *See also* homeless; homelessness
Poverty-housing syndrome, 35
Poverty line, 13, 14
Powell Place, 40, 89
Price, Gordon, 96
Privatization, 195-200. *See also* Great Britain: privatization
Pro-Canada Network, 119, 125
Public housing, 53, 135-36, 195, 199-200; privatization, 195-200

Quebec, homelessness, 52

Racism, 46, 138-39. *See also* Discrimination
Real estate development, 58, 75, 86; world's most expensive, 132. *See also* Downtown eastside hotels; Land development; Land speculation
Real estate marketplace, 163
Redway, Alan, 118, 135-37
Refugees. *See* Homeless, immigrants and refugees
Rent: percentage paid by low income earners, 208
Rent controls, 16, 56, 118
Rent increases, 16, 17, 39, 79, 92-93, 117-18
Rent regulation system, request for, 92, 96
Rental housing: adult only, 16, 35, 39, 147, 171, 177, 184-91, 211; decrease in, 14, 93; portion of units available (in greater Vancouver) rents near maximum GAIN shelter allowance, 169(table). *See also* Demolition of hotels and housing; Discrimination in housing; Downtown eastside hotels; Secondary suite closures; Social Credit government, promises of new rental housing; Vacancy rate
Rental housing starts, 88
Rental housing subsidies, 187
Rentalsperson: NDP pushes for return, 118
Residential hotels and rooming houses. *See* Downtown eastside hotels
Residential Tenancy Act. *See* B.C. Residential Tenancy Act
Residential Tenancy Branch, 29, 191
Richmond, Claude, 195, 196
Rogers, Stephen, 196, 197
Rooming houses. *See* Downtown eastside hotels; *See also under* name of rooming house, e.g. Ohio Rooms, etc.
Ross, Aileen, 120
Runaway children, 173-74. *See also* Homeless, children and youth

St. James Social Service Society, 206n.

Salvation Army, 36, 76
SAVE (Squatters Alliance of Vancouver East), 76, 79-80, 84, press statement from, 79
Secondary suite closures, 16, 47, 93, 95, 118, 186; request for moratorium on, 92, 96
Secondary suite permits, 162
Secondary suite review policy, 93
Seniors, 53
Seniors' housing, 204
Shanahan, Noreen, 184
Shared accommodation, 17
Shayler, John, 186
Shelter, adequate; definition of, 10
Shelterless. *See* Homelessness
Shelterless Committee Newsletter, 28-31
Shelters. *See* Emergency Shelters. *See also under* name of Shelter, e.g. Crosswalk, Lookout, Powell Place, Triage, etc.
Sigurgeirson, Mugs, 165, 167, 170
Silver Lodge, 63, 109
Single Displaced Persons' Project (Toronto), 8n., 207n.
Single Mothers, 17, 32-36, 38-9, 42, 89-90, 116, 138-39, 143-44, 147-48, 171-72, 182-91. *See also* Homeless; Downtown eastside hotels; Women and abuse
Skalbania, Nelson, 196
Smith, Peter, 126n.
Snyder, Mitch, 131
Social Credit government, 94, 195-200; promises of new rental housing, 95. *See also* Privatization
Social housing, 42, 47, 50, 79, 91; privatization, 195-200. *See also* Public housing
Social Services and Housing, Ministry of, 60, 64, 140-43; Bed Index, 31; blames homeless, 34; three-year plan, 195. *See also* Emergency Services
Soeurs Grises de Montreal, 123. *See also* Montreal, Grey Nuns
SPARC (Social Planning and Research Council of British Columbia, 167n.
Squat Hop, 84
Squatters and Squatting, 16, 45, 72-88, 91, 93, 98,; in Denmark, 87; in England, 87; in New York, 85;

INDEX

philosophy, 75, 85, 87; support for, 84; in West Germany, 87. *See also* Frances Street Squatters
Stannard, Helen, 31
Stannard, Laura, 29, 191
Strathcona Community Health Team, 26
Strathcona Gardens, 104, 167; homeless living in, 167, 169-70
Strathcona Park, 169; homeless living in, 167-70
Street kids: statistics, 174; *See also* Homeless, children and youth; Street youth
Street people. *See* homeless; homelessness
Street youth: number of street youth by type and gender, 175(table); *See also* Homeless, children and youth; Street kids
Swanson, Jean, 208

Taylor, Carol, 91, 118
Taylor, Gordon, 30
Taylor, Paul, 100
Tenant protection, 209
Tenants, militant, 117
Tenants Rights Coalition, 14, 162n., 186, 191, 188, 208
Tenants Rights Hotline, 14
Tent city, Vancouver, 150
Thatcher, Margaret, 195-97, 199. *See also* Great Britain, privatization
Thomas, Peter, 196, 199, 200
Third World homeless. *See* World homeless
Timmins, Leslie, 170
Toronto: emergency shelter-statistics, 127; gentrification, 126; homelessness, 51; statistics, 51, 126-27
Transsexuals, 35, 49, 60
Triage Shelter, 26, 28, 31, 142
Tully, Karen, 39
Turvey, John, 30, 48, 183

Unemployment: effect of inflation on, 13; and interest rates, 13; statistics, 13
United Nations Centre for Human Settlements (Habitat), 10n.
United States: affordable housing loss, 131; gentrification, 74; homeless and homelessness, 7, 42, 47, 55, 128-31; housing programs, 129

Urban Core Shelterless Committee, 51

Vacancy rates, 14, 51(table), 118, 186
Vancouver and District Public Housing Tenants Association, 53, 195
Vancouver City Charter, 96
Vancouver City Council, 92, 93, 94, 96
Vancouver City Hall Demonstration, (May 1, 1990), 91; demands of protestors, 92, 96; statement read to City Council, 92-96
Vancouver City "initiatives" to deal with housing market, 95
Vancouver City Police, 161-62. *See also* Frances Street Squatters
Vancouver Detox Centre, 28, 31
Vancouver General Hospital, 28, 31
Vancouver Housing Registry. *See* YWCA Vancouver Housing Registry
Vancouver Land Corporation, 85, 95
Vancouver Police Department, 28
Vancouver Social Planning department, 175
Vander Zalm, Bill, 71
Victory House, 65

Wages: decline in, 13. *See also* Minimum wage
Washington Hotel, 26
Welfare rates, 3(table), 36, 55, 56, 147
Wenham, Diane, 31
West End, Vancouver, 117
Wilson, Alan, 131n.
Women and abuse, 17, 33, 41, 56, 90, 100, 108, 116, 119, 120, 139, 147
Women's Housing Manifesto, 42-43
World homelesss, statistics, 131

Year of the Woman, 119
Yee, Ning, 73, 82, 83, 84
YWCA (Young Women's Christian Assocation), 24, 174
YWCA Hotel, 137-39
YWCA Vancouver Housing Registry, 137, 139, 170-72, 184

Sheila Baxter is a single mother of five children, a single grandmother of eight grandchildren, a tutor of English at Carnegie Centre, a writer and poet, a member of End Legislated Poverty, a member of the Carnegie Association. She has lived for seven years with Fred, a white Angora cat, and has worked in the anti-poverty movement for sixteen years or more.

"Even though I have been abused and homeless—I HAVE SURVIVED. I finished high school. In my middle years I went to Langara College, successfully took eight courses. I have never been a substance abuser.

"When I was a single parent I worked as a community worker and supported my family. Now I am a writer—a street poet, and tutor.

"I struggle daily with oppression and refuse to accept the growing trend of professional opinions that say you should be *this* because of *that*. We don't have to accept labels."

Printed in Canada